Will Rogers

WILL ROGERS
Cherokee Entertainer

Liz Sonneborn

Senior Consulting Editor
W. David Baird
Howard A. White Professor of History
Pepperdine University

CHELSEA HOUSE PUBLISHERS

New York   Philadelphia

FRONTISPIECE   Will Rogers as he was photographed on the eve of his
fateful last flight in 1935.

ON THE COVER   An illustration by Vilma Ortiz shows Will Rogers performing one of the rope tricks with which he delighted audiences on
theater stages across America.

Chelsea House Publishers
EDITORIAL DIRECTOR   Richard Scott Rennert
EXECUTIVE MANAGING EDITOR   Karyn Gullen Browne
EXECUTIVE EDITOR   Sean Dolan
COPY CHIEF   Robin James
PICTURE EDITOR   Adrian G. Allen
MANUFACTURING DIRECTOR   Gerald Levine
SYSTEMS MANAGER   Lindsey Ottman
PRODUCTION COORDINATOR   Marie Claire Cebrián-Ume

North American Indians of Achievement
SENIOR EDITOR   Sean Dolan

Staff for WILL ROGERS
COPY EDITOR   Margaret Dornfeld
EDITORIAL ASSISTANTS   Nicole Greenblatt, Joy Sanchez
SENIOR DESIGNER   Rae Grant
PICTURE RESEARCHER   Wendy P. Wills
COVER ILLUSTRATOR   Vilma Ortiz

Printed and bound in Mexico.

First Printing

1   3   5   7   9   8   6   4   2

Library of Congress Cataloging-in-Publication Data

Sonneborn, Liz.
Will Rogers, Cherokee entertainer/Liz Sonneborn.
   p. cm.
Includes bibliographical references and index.
ISBN 0-7910-1719-2
ISBN 0-7910-1988-8 (pbk.)
1. Rogers, Will, 1879–1935—Juvenile literature. 2. Entertainers—United States—
Biography—Juvenile literature. 3. Humorists, American—Biography—Juvenile
literature. I. Title.

PN2287.R74S66 1993   92-45050
792.7'028'092—dc20   CIP
[B]

CONTENTS

NORTH AMERICAN INDIANS OF ACHIEVEMENT

BLACK HAWK
Sac Rebel

JOSEPH BRANT
Mohawk Chief

COCHISE
Apache Chief

CRAZY HORSE
Sioux War Chief

CHIEF GALL
Sioux War Chief

GERONIMO
Apache Warrior

HIAWATHA
Founder of the Iroquois
Confederacy

CHIEF JOSEPH
Nez Perce Leader

PETER MacDONALD
Former Chairman of the Navajo
Nation

WILMA MANKILLER
Principal Chief of the Cherokees

OSCEOLA
Seminole Rebel

QUANAH PARKER
Comanche Chief

KING PHILIP
Wampanoag Rebel

POCAHONTAS
Powhatan Peacemaker

PONTIAC
Ottawa Rebel

RED CLOUD
Sioux War Chief

WILL ROGERS
Cherokee Entertainer

SEQUOYAH
Inventor of the Cherokee Alphabet

SITTING BULL
Chief of the Sioux

TECUMSEH
Shawnee Rebel

JIM THORPE
Sac and Fox Athlete

SARAH WINNEMUCCA
Northern Paiute Writer and
Diplomat

Other titles in preparation

ON INDIAN LEADERSHIP

by W. David Baird
Howard A. White Professor of History
Pepperdine University

Authoritative utterance is in thy mouth, perception is in thy heart, and thy tongue is the shrine of justice," the ancient Egyptians said of their king. From him, the Egyptians expected authority, discretion, and just behavior. Homer's *Iliad* suggests that the Greeks demanded somewhat different qualities from their leaders: justice and judgment, wisdom and counsel, shrewdness and cunning, valor and action. It is not surprising that different people living at different times should seek different qualities from the individuals they looked to for guidance. By and large, a people's requirements for leadership are determined by two factors: their culture and the unique circumstances of the time and place in which they live.

Before the late 15th century, when non-Indians first journeyed to what is now North America, most Indian tribes were not ruled by a single person. Instead, there were village chiefs, clan headmen, peace chiefs, war chiefs, and a host of other types of leaders, each with his or her own specific duties. These influential people not only decided political matters but also helped shape their tribe's social, cultural, and religious life. Usually, Indian leaders held their positions because they had won the respect of their peers. Indeed, if a leader's followers at any time decided that he or she was out of step with the will of the people, they felt free to look to someone else for advice and direction.

Thus, the greatest achievers in traditional Indian communities were men and women of extraordinary talent. They were not only skilled at navigating the deadly waters of tribal politics and cultural customs but also able to, directly or indirectly, make a positive and significant difference in the daily life of their followers.

From the beginning of their interaction with Native Americans, non-Indians failed to understand these features of Indian leadership. Early European explorers and settlers merely assumed that Indians had the same relationship with their leaders as non-Indians had with their kings and queens. European monarchs generally inherited their positions and ruled large nations however they chose, often with little regard for the desires or needs of their subjects. As a result, the settlers of Jamestown saw Pocahontas as a "princess" and Pilgrims dubbed Wampanoag leader Metacom "King Philip," envisioning them in roles very different from those in which their own people placed them.

As more and more non-Indians flocked to North America, the nature of Indian leadership gradually began to change. Influential Indians no longer had to take on the often considerable burden of pleasing only their own people; they also had to develop a strategy of dealing with the non-Indian newcomers. In a rapidly changing world, new types of Indian role models with new ideas and talents continually emerged. Some were warriors; others were peacemakers. Some held political positions within their tribes; others were writers, artists, religious prophets, or athletes. Although the demands of Indian leadership altered from generation to generation, several factors that determined which Indian people became prominent in the centuries after first contact remained the same.

Certain personal characteristics distinguished these Indians of achievement. They were intelligent, imaginative, practical, daring, shrewd, uncompromising, ruthless, and logical. They were constant in friendships, unrelenting in hatreds, affectionate with their relatives, and respectful to their God or gods. Of course, no single Native American leader embodied all these qualities, nor these qualities only. But it was these characteristics that allowed them to succeed.

The special skills and talents that certain Indians possessed also brought them to positions of importance. The life of Hiawatha, the legendary founder of the powerful Iroquois Confederacy, displays the value that oratorical ability had for many Indians in power.

The biography of Cochise, the 19th-century Apache chief, illustrates that leadership often required keen diplomatic skills not only in transactions among tribespeople but also in hardheaded negotiations with non-Indians. For others, such as Mohawk Joseph Brant and Navajo Peter MacDonald, a non-Indian education proved advantageous in their dealings with other peoples.

Sudden changes in circumstance were another crucial factor in determining who became influential in Indian communities. King Philip in the 1670s and Geronimo in the 1880s both came to power when their people were searching for someone to lead them into battle against white frontiersmen who had forced upon them a long series of indignities. Seeing the rising discontent of Indians of many tribes in the 1810s, Tecumseh and his brother, the Shawnee prophet Tenskwatawa, proclaimed a message of cultural revitalization that appealed to thousands. Other Indian achievers recognized cooperation with non-Indians as the most advantageous path during their lifetime. Sarah Winnemucca in the late 19th century bridged the gap of understanding between her people and their non-Indian neighbors through the publication of her autobiography *Life Among the Piutes*. Olympian Jim Thorpe in the early 20th century championed the assimilationist policies of the U.S. government and, with his own successes, demonstrated the accomplishments Indians could make in the non-Indian world. And Wilma Mankiller, principal chief of the Cherokees, continues to fight successfully for the rights of her people through the courts and through negotiation with federal officials.

Leadership among Native Americans, just as among all other peoples, can be understood only in the context of culture and history. But the centuries that Indians have had to cope with invasions of foreigners in their homelands have brought unique hardships and obstacles to the Native American individuals who most influenced and inspired others. Despite these challenges, there has never been a lack of Indian men and women equal to these tasks. With such strong leaders, it is no wonder that Native Americans remain such a vital part of this nation's cultural landscape.

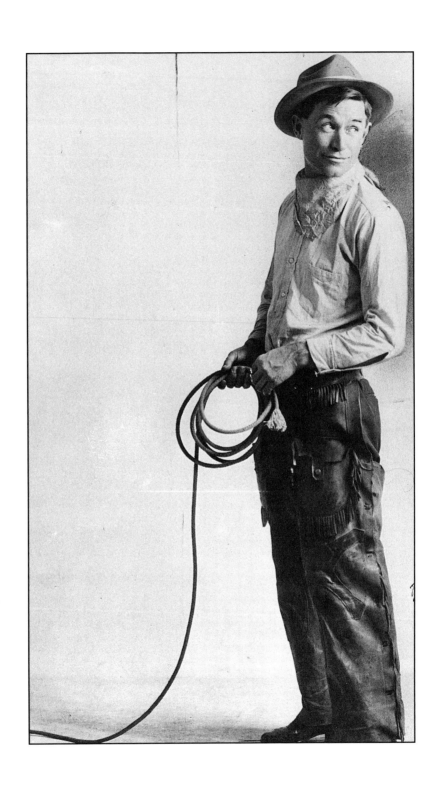

1

THE COWBOY PHILOSOPHER

Gene Buck was not a happy man that day in 1915. As he sat in his office, shuffling papers from one side of his desk to the other, he tried to keep his mind on his work, but he was having little success. He was dreading the meeting he was about to have, and his mind was far too occupied.

Meetings like this were part of his job, Buck knew, part of show business. Unavoidable and sad, they were the one aspect of his work he absolutely hated. Usually he loved what he did for a living, which was work side by side with the greatest theater producer alive.

His boss, Florenz Ziegfeld, Jr., was a legend, largely because of the *Ziegfeld Follies*. Performed nightly at the New Amsterdam Theater in New York City, the show was known throughout the world. Its lavish sets and costumes were unmatched anywhere. Its performers, especially the dancers, were equally unrivaled. The *Ziegfeld Follies* was known as the home of the most beautiful show girls in the world.

Few would dispute that Ziegfeld was a theatrical genius, but Buck knew that he had his blind spots. His boss had a great eye for lovely women and spectacular sets, but other types of acts held little appeal for Ziegfeld, and he never quite understood why his audience was

Although he was extremely proud of his Native American heritage, Will Rogers helped define the popular conception of the cowboy.

clamoring for a little more variety in the show. To him, beautiful show girls *were* the *Follies*. Other acts were useful only as fillers while the women were offstage changing their costumes.

Buck tried to provide Ziegfeld with a different viewpoint. He was always on the lookout for new talent to add to the nightly revue at the New Amsterdam. Although Ziegfeld was often initially unenthusiastic about Buck's finds, he had learned to trust his assistant, who seemed to have a feel for what the *Follies* audience would like.

Usually, Buck was grateful for his boss's confidence in him. But that day, as he sat at his desk nervously drumming his fingers against its surface, he almost regretted it. Ziegfeld's faith in Buck had gotten him into a miserable fix. Any minute, one of Buck's latest discoveries, a young man named Will Rogers, was going to come through the door, and Buck would have to perform the unhappy task of firing him.

Buck had first seen Rogers perform only a few weeks earlier, when he had gone to another theater on one of his frequent hunts for new talent. The show that was playing, a musical revue called *Hands Up*, was disappointing, full of lavish, flashy but ultimately boring numbers—pale imitations of the kind of thing the *Ziegfeld Follies* did so much better. But near the end of the program, as Buck was thinking about leaving the theater, something caught his attention.

Onto the stage ambled a friendly-faced, tousled-haired man wearing a cowboy getup and carrying a collection of lassos in his hand. He smiled at the audience, then threw out one of the ropes, twirling it in a circle in preparation for one of the complicated rope tricks he was hired to perform. But as he went into the trick, he miscalculated the size of the small stage, and the rope

Like many other successful entertainers, Rogers often had to act as his own promoter. He had these cards, advertising his skill with the lariat and as a trick rider, printed at his own expense.

The Greatest Catch in Vaudeville

Manipulating 90 ft of Rope.

COMPLIMENTS OF   **WILL ROGERS,**   THE LARIET EXPERT

whacked into the backdrop and fell to the ground with a loud thud. The audience was silent as the obviously embarrassed cowboy reached down and picked it up. Without a word, he tried the trick a second time. Again, the rope slammed loudly onto the stage floor.

Show directors had a standard way of dealing with such disasters—get the performer away from the audience as fast as possible, or "give 'em the hook" in theater parlance. As the curtain came down on the rope twirler, Buck thought sadly that the curtain had probably been drawn on the young hopeful's theater career.

To his surprise, the audience was thinking differently. Instead of hurling jeers and catcalls, people here and there began to clap, and soon the entire theater was filled with the sound of applause. The curtain went back up, but when the audience saw another musical number was next, they booed and hooted, demanding the return of the clumsy cowboy. They did not care that he had botched his act—there was something so appealing about him that the audience just wanted to see more of him.

The Ziegfeld Follies were renowned for their fanciful production numbers, like this one entitled "Children's Toy Number."

The curtain went back down; after a few tense moments, it rose again as the cowboy, his smile even broader this time out, sauntered back onstage. The act went well this time, and the audience responded with a standing ovation. Buck was impressed. It did not take too much imagination to recognize that he had found a real crowd pleaser.

Still, it required just the kind of imagination that Ziegfeld lacked. When Buck told him he wanted to hire a lariat-twirling cowboy named Will Rogers for his beloved *Follies*, Ziegfeld looked at his assistant as though he were crazy. Why anyone would want to feature some dirty, uncouth, drawling cowboy on the same stage as his beauties was beyond him.

Though it took some time, Ziegfeld finally came around to Buck's idea. He let Buck hire Rogers for the *Midnight Frolic*, a show that came on every night after the *Follies*. The *Frolic* was not as prestigious or popular as its predecessor, but it had a loyal following among the most fashionable men and women in New York society.

For his first few weeks with the *Frolic*, Rogers performed well but was far from the sensation Buck had hoped. His act consisted of a few rope tricks interspersed with a few jokes, most of which Rogers made up on the spot. Improvising new humorous material night after night was not easy, and Rogers adopted the habit of scanning the crowd for someone famous he could gently and good-naturedly tease—a surefire way to delight the rest of his audience. Unfortunately, when he could not find anyone, Rogers tended to make Ziegfeld the butt of his gibes.

Not known for his sense of humor, Ziegfeld rarely found Rogers's playful digs at all funny. He was especially annoyed when Rogers announced one night to his audience, "I am going to stick with this fellow Ziegfeld

. . . I am off all the shows that go in for art." To Ziegfeld, the *Frolic* was most definitely art, and if Rogers could not see that, he did not belong in the show. Midway through Rogers's second week, Ziegfeld decided he had had enough. He told Buck that he was going on a trip for a week; when he returned, he wanted the cowboy gone.

Once his boss had departed, a sad Buck asked Rogers to come to his office for a brief meeting. Buck hated firing any performer, but it was even worse with Rogers. He liked the cowboy, and besides, Rogers had taken the job in the first place only at Buck's urging.

In a few minutes, Rogers came in, wearing a smile as always and extending his customary greeting, "I'm glad to see you, Mr. Buck." While the producer took a deep breath, readying himself to deliver the bad news, Rogers blurted out the last thing Buck expected to hear: "I want fifty a week more."

Buck paused. Slightly embarrassed, he asked Rogers why he thought he should get a raise. Rogers said he needed the money for his family, then quickly added that he also had a new idea for making his act better. "My wife says I ought to talk about what I read in the papers," he explained. "She says I'm always reading the papers, so why not pass along what I read."

Rogers was eager to try out her suggestion, he explained to the increasingly nonplussed Buck. He had recognized that his act had not really caught on with the *Frolic* audience, and he thought he knew why: Almost half of the people who came to the show on any given night were regulars. "A man won't laugh at the same joke more than once," Rogers explained, so he had to keep coming up with new material. If he concentrated on current events, he figured he would have a fresh batch of subjects to talk about every night—subjects with which every member of his audience would likely be familiar.

In the Follies, *Rogers often played the role of a reluctant and innocent cowboy pursued by beautiful women.*

At first, Buck was not enthusiastic. If Rogers were planning on attacking prominent and powerful people, like politicians, Ziegfeld would not like it. Besides, it could get everyone into a lot of legal trouble. Rogers assured Buck his jokes would be about only the most well-known public figures, people so famous that they had to be fair game.

Barely able to believe what he heard himself saying, Buck told the man he had been about to fire only moments before that the new act sounded good, though he maintained enough self-control to explain to Rogers that he would have to wait a week for a decision about his salary. By that time, Buck hoped, he would have devised some way of explaining it all to Ziegfeld.

Uncertain of exactly what he had gotten himself into, Buck made a point of watching the *Frolic* that night. When Rogers first came onstage, his act looked unchanged. There he was, the same old Will, wearing his cowboy boots and hat, an old bandanna tied around his neck and a rope in his hand. As usual, he began twirling the rope and then speaking in a soft, drawling voice that immediately informed his audience that he had been raised far from their high-society circles. Nonchalantly watching the rope, almost as though he himself had nothing to do with its constant snaky motion, he spoke calmly, seeming to say whatever came into his head without giving it a second thought.

Tonight, though, Buck soon realized, there *was* something different about Rogers. He was wearing his usual costume, charming his audience in his usual way, but now he was not just chatting about the people watching his act or repeating a joke that had come to him a few days ago. At last, he had something of real substance to talk about. And Buck saw for the first time that it was not just the homespun way Rogers said something that was getting the laughs. It was his unique way of seeing the world that the audience was responding to.

Rogers's subject that night was a news story that had been treated by the press with the utmost solemnity. With World War I raging in Europe and the debate about the United States's potential role in the conflict intensifying at home, Henry Ford, the industrialist who had become one of the world's richest men by manufacturing the Model T automobile, had just launched his own highly publicized effort to achieve peace. He proposed sending a delegation of pacifists to Holland, where he expected them to negotiate with the world's leaders to halt the fighting. To Rogers, the idea so smacked of arrogance that he could not resist giving the automobile maker a ribbing.

"See where Henry Ford's peace ship has landed in Holland," Rogers drawled to the audience. Twirling his rope constantly, he continued with his slangy, gentle sarcasm:

> Ford's all wrong, instead of taking a lot of them high-powered fellers on his ship, he should've hired away all these Ziegfeld pippins [show girls]. He'd not only got the boys out of the trenches by Christmas but he'd have Kaiser Bill [Wilhelm II, the emperor of Germany] and Lloyd George [the prime minister of England] and Clemenceau [the premier of France] shootin' craps to see which one'd head the line at the stage door.

The audience howled. His joke was funny and affectionate but also struck a serious chord that made the audience laugh all the more. Rogers used laughter to express the loss of faith in political leaders—who had plunged much of the world into a bloody, and possibly senseless, war—that many people were feeling.

As he had been the first time he had seen Rogers perform, Buck was impressed, though he now saw that

Florenz Ziegfeld became a legend as a show business impresario through his creation of the Ziegfeld Follies, *an elaborate theatrical revue that owed its popularity primarily to the display of shapely female figures.*

maybe even he had not been giving the cowboy enough credit. Rogers proved that night that he was more than an engaging performer who knew how to ingratiate himself to an audience. He was a shrewd man who could use his folksy character and wit to say important things that people were interested in hearing but were perhaps too frightened or uninformed to articulate themselves.

Buck grew even more pleased as the week continued and he watched Rogers grow increasingly comfortable with his new stage persona. He was even happier with the audience's reaction. The regulars at the *Frolic* loved Rogers and his willingness to poke fun at anyone or anything that deserved it.

Though Buck was now convinced that Rogers was destined to become a *Frolic* star, he was less sure that he could persuade Ziegfeld that the cowboy was worth keeping on. As soon as he returned to New York, Ziegfeld called his assistant to find out what had happened at the theater in his absence. One of his first questions was, "How did your cowboy friend take it when you fired him?" The great showman was not pleased by Buck's answer. "Come hear him tonight," Buck replied, "and then if you want to fire him, do it yourself."

Ziegfeld showed up for the *Frolic* that night. He found little about Will's routine amusing, but to a master showman like Ziegfeld the audience's laughter sounded like a cash register ringing. It meant profits, and more shows, and even greater profits in the future. Although Ziegfeld considered himself an artist, he was above all else a businessman. He did not have to like Rogers and his act to recognize that the young performer before him was a gold mine. Somewhat angrily, he told Buck what his assistant had hoped to hear. "We'll keep him another week," the great Ziegfeld choked out. Neither Ziegfeld nor even Buck could have possibly guessed that the cowboy philosopher they had agreed to keep on would one day become one of America's most beloved performers.

2

GROWING UP CHEROKEE

In the course of Will Rogers's lifetime, most Americans came to regard the native peoples of their country as a vanishing race. Robbed of their land and, in the case of reservation residents, their freedom, Indians had little political or economic power and were hence easily ignored by the non-Indian majority of the United States. To Rogers, though, the Indian world was always alive and well. When, in the eyes of many, he came to represent quintessential American values, it only seemed just to him. After all, as a Cherokee he was descended from the very first Americans. "My ancestors didn't come on the *Mayflower*," he often said, "but they met the boat."

William Penn Adair Rogers was born on November 4, 1879, in Indian Territory, an area of land that would later be incorporated into the state of Oklahoma. He inherited Cherokee blood from both his mother and his father. "My father was one-eighth Cherokee Indian and my mother was a quarter-blood Cherokee," he once explained. "I never got far enough in arithmetic to figure out how much injun that made me, but there's nothing of which I am more proud than my Cherokee blood."

Although in the above instances Will Rogers spoke of his Cherokee heritage in a light vein—as he always spoke of everything in public—Rogers knew the history of the

Rogers as a student at Kemper Military Academy in Booneville, Missouri. An indifferent student at best, he seldom took as much pride in his classwork as he did in his uniform.

Cherokee Indians and had learned many lessons from it. Perhaps the unfair and cruel treatment that the Cherokees had received from the United States government helped form his strong sense of justice and fairness. It probably contributed as well to his healthy skepticism about politics and government.

At the time of his birth, the Cherokees' history in the West had been relatively short. Until only about 40 years earlier, they had lived in a large, lush territory in the southern Appalachians, covering much of the present-day states of North and South Carolina, Georgia, Alabama, Tennessee, Virginia, and Kentucky. The fertility of their land and their skill as farmers allowed them to prosper and their population to grow. When the Spanish explorer Hernando de Soto, in 1540, became the first non-Indian to meet the Cherokees, they probably numbered almost 25,000, making them one of the largest southeastern tribes.

In the 18th century, the Cherokees encountered many more whites as English and Scottish traders started to establish posts in their territory. Attracted both by the richness of the land and the hospitality of the people, some decided to spend their lives among the Cherokees. Most of these men married Cherokee women. The offspring of these marriages added a new element to the Cherokee population—mixed bloods, as people with Indian and white ancestry became known. Within several generations, the majority of Cherokees were mixed bloods. (Rogers's ancestry can be traced back to European traders on both sides of his family tree.)

The white traders brought other changes to Cherokee society. From them, the tribe obtained new types of goods. In time, cloth garments and metal tools from Europe replaced the deerskin clothing and bone implements the Indians had long made by hand.

This baby picture of "Willie" Rogers, as he was known in his youth, is the earliest portrait of one of the most frequently photographed individuals of his day.

Although the Cherokees had their own rich culture, they were willing to adopt whatever elements of the British way of life appealed to them. For instance, some Cherokees began to convert to the Christian religion and learn to read, write, and speak English. Eventually, the Cherokees' way of life was almost identical to the intruders'. The only significant differences were the result of the Cherokees' excellent school system, which made the Indians better educated than many of the settlers.

Unfortunately, their adoption of white ways did not benefit the Cherokees when white settlers decided they wanted the Indians' land. Pressured by the settlers in Cherokee territory, in 1830 the U.S. Congress passed legislation—the Indian Removal Act—that spelled doom for the tribe. The act stated that the president could negotiate with any eastern Indian tribe for their reloca-

This 19th-century political cartoon portrays the Cherokee nation as a once-proud and powerful giant brought down, bound, and carved up by a combination of political and commercial interests. Uncle Sam, perched on the prone Indian's nose, presides benignly over the tragedy.

tion (removal) to lands west of the Mississippi River. Many Indian tribes had already been removed, so technically the legislation did not give the president any new power. The true intent of the act was to inform all concerned that the federal government considered the removal of all eastern Indians to be inevitable.

Though the Cherokees were certainly alarmed by the Indian Removal Act, many refused to believe that the president, Andrew Jackson, despite his proven hostility to Indians, would actually compel them to leave their homes. (Jackson had led troops against both the Creeks and the Seminoles, who with the Choctaws, Chickasaws, and the Cherokees constituted the so-called Five Civilized Tribes of the Southeast.) After all, the Cherokees were, by white standards, already "civilized."

A small group of Cherokees, however, figured that it was only a matter of time before the government forced them out of their homeland. When, in 1836, the government scheduled the Cherokees' removal for two years later, they decided that the sooner they made the move the better off they would be. These refugees packed up their belongings and set off for Indian Territory, the designated homeland for removed Indians, which included portions of present-day Oklahoma, Arkansas, and Missouri. These first Cherokees to arrive in Indian Territory became known as Old Settlers.

The majority of the Cherokees remained in their homeland, hoping to persuade the United States to allow them to stay in the land of their ancestors. But the inevitable occurred, and in 1838 the U.S. Army led the tribe on its tragic western exodus. Though the government had promised to feed the Cherokees on their march, their provisions were rancid and paltry. Weakened, starving, traveling hundreds of miles on foot in the dead of winter, the Cherokees began to fall ill. Dysentery,

Elizabeth Hunt Gunter Schrimsher, Rogers's grandmother, the mother of Mary America. She was approximately one-half Cherokee. Rogers himself was just over a quarter Cherokee; the rest was Scottish and Irish.

measles, and whooping cough took thousands of lives. Behind them, the emigrants left a row of graves, marking their long route west. By the time the Cherokees arrived in Indian Territory, one-fourth of their population was dead. Now known as the Trail of Tears, the Cherokees' removal is one of the most tragic and shameful events in U.S. history. The Indian tribe that had adopted more "civilized," white lifeways than any other was treated no better—and in some ways more harshly—by the American government than any other Native American people.

One of the most influential architects of the new Cherokee Nation was Robert Rogers, an Old Settler and mixed blood who had been among the first Cherokees to arrive in Indian Territory, most likely in 1836. In only a few years, he had built a log house for himself and his wife, a mixed blood named Sallie Vann, and had found a new profession—ranching. Although the land in Indian Territory was almost impossible to farm, it was ideal for maintaining cattle. Vast areas were covered with grass on which herds of cattle could graze.

In 1839, one year before Robert's death, Sallie gave birth to a son, whom they named Clem. As a boy, Clem attended one of the schools that the Cherokees immediately established in the Territory. Although the education he was offered was of a much higher quality than that available in most American schools, the boy did not care for his studies. When his mother remarried, Clem, then 17, quit school and decided to strike out on his own.

With Sallie's gift of 25 longhorn cattle, Clem set out for the Coowescoowee district in the northeastern corner of the Cherokee Nation. Like his father, the young man had a knack for ranching, and his business prospered. In a few years, he had earned enough money to marry, and he proposed to Mary America Schrimsher, a tall young

woman of Cherokee, Dutch, and Welsh descent. Warm and witty, with a temperament far gentler than Clem's, Mary saw courage and intelligence in her gruff beau and happily agreed to become his wife.

By the time Will, the last of his parents' eight children, was born, his father had established himself as a successful rancher, despite having had to start over after the Cherokee Indians were punished by the destruction of their property for having sided—under strong pressure from the Confederacy—with the South in the Civil War. His V-shaped spread, ideally situated between the Caney and Verdigris rivers, well watered, and covered with wild bluegrass, was one of the most profitable ranches in the territory, and everyone for miles around knew the distinctive CV brand of Clem Vann Rogers. The family—only Will and his sisters Sallie, Maud, and May (or Mae) survived childhood—lived in one of the grandest homes in Indian Territory, a large, two-story house with lace curtains and the only piano for miles around. Hospitable by nature, Mary loved to invite neighbors and travelers over for a night of singing and dancing.

As a young boy, Will learned to love ranch life. He knew little about the actual work expected of cowboys, of course—the dangers of the roundup of longhorn steers each spring in Texas, the long days and nights of the cattle drive to the ranch and then the stockyards, the loneliness and tedium of patrolling the range, the rough-and-tumble of branding—but he greatly enjoyed the freedom and fun of riding and roping, his two favorite forms of play. His closest companion was Uncle Dan Walker, a black cowboy who worked for Clem. Uncle

Rogers was born in this large prairie farmhouse, which his father had built on the Verdigris River. The home was known as the White House; owing to Clem Rogers's importance in the community, it was regularly the site of government and business meetings as well as social gatherings.

Mary America Schrimsher, Will Rogers's mother, was a gentle woman who used humor to disarm her husband's quick temper. She died when Will was just 10; his father tried to relieve the boy's grief by giving him a pony.

Dan patiently showed the boy again and again how to throw a rope and, as Will began to catch on, how to perform a few simple rope tricks to impress his sisters. Will loved roping, and anything that moved became fair game.

This idyllic time ended when Will was six and his father decided that it was time for him to go to school. Education was always a priority for Cherokee parents, but young Will did not share Mary and Clem's enthusiasm. He hated being cooped up indoors when he could be spending his time with cowboys and horses. When it became clear that Will was not much of a student, his parents decided he should change schools. Before long, they received a note from the principal of Will's new school tactfully suggesting that perhaps everyone would be better off if the boy came home.

Sadly, Will's return did not bring him back to the happy, carefree life he associated with the ranch. In the summer of 1890, his mother fell ill with dysentery and died. For the rest of his life, Will would mourn her loss. Years later, he told his fans that he had inherited his sense of humor from this lively, fun-loving woman.

Over Will's protests, Clem decided that the boy still needed to continue his education. He was sent off to various boarding schools, only to be sent home from each one for his lack of interest in his books and his fascination with roping. He spent most of his time happily improving his skill with the lariat and roping goats, wild turkeys, and coyotes. One school gave up on Will when, on a dare, he tried to rope the headmaster's horse and instead frightened the skittery animal into a panic. After racing through the school's tennis court, the horse ran off and was never seen again.

Only Kemper Military School in Boonville, Missouri, seemed to agree with Will. Clem hoped that the discipline of a military school would whip his boy into shape, but Will enjoyed the school mostly because he liked his military uniform, which he always wore proudly on visits home. However, he did learn to like a few of his subjects as well. He made good marks in history and showed a flare for elocution, which involved making speeches in front of his class. No matter what he was reciting, he always tried to please his audience with his performance. One classmate remembered later that "he'd torture his face till it looked like a wrinkled saddle blanket, make funny motions with his hands and roll his eyes and, some way or other, manage to make us laugh. I never saw him get up in front of a class without making them laugh before he sat down."

Will spent two years at Kemper before the inevitable boredom made him decide to give up on education altogether. Without telling his father, he set out, at age 18, to find work as a cowboy. For a few months he worked for a friend of his father's in Higgins, Texas, and then moved on to Amarillo. There he took a job on a big ranch, where, to his delight, he watched and learned from cowhands with plenty of experience handling big herds. After a brief visit home and a cool reception from an angry Clem, he worked his way to present-day New Mexico and then California.

In San Francisco, Rogers ran into trouble that temporarily ended his travels and almost ended his life. He and another cowboy were sharing a room in a small hotel. When they went to sleep, Rogers's roommate "blew out" the flame of the room's gas light. The two young men were accustomed to kerosene lamps, in which the

As a young man, Rogers loved to socialize. Here, he and best friend Spi Trent (right) are dressed up for an outing with the McClellan sisters, Mary (left) and Pearl.

kerosene fuel stopped burning as soon as the flame was extinguished. However, the gas emitted from a gas light continues to be released until a valve is turned to shut it off. As Rogers and his friend slept, gas filled their room. The two young men were found unconscious. Rogers was raced to a hospital where the emergency-room doctor abandoned him for dead. Fortunately, some medical students who happened to be present decided to experiment on him, trying out various unorthodox techniques of treatment. In the end Rogers revived.

When he had recovered enough to travel, Will returned to Clem's ranch. By his own account, he "landed home in pretty bad shape" following his close encounter with death, and his father urged him to stay close to home for a while. Will was still restless, though, and Indian Territory was not the same place it had been when he had left only two years earlier.

In 1898, Congress passed the Curtis Act, which abolished one of the Cherokees' most valued traditions—holding their land in common. The land of the Cherokee Nation was thought to belong to all Cherokees. If someone wanted to start a farm or a ranch, he could claim any unoccupied tract. He was free to use the claimed land for as long as he needed it, but he was not thought of as its owner. If he vacated the land, any other Cherokee was free to move onto it without paying for anything but the improvements the previous occupant had made. This system had allowed Clem to prosper as a rancher. As his ranch grew, he merely claimed whatever land he needed to expand his operation. At its height, the Rogers ranch stretched over 60,000 acres.

The Curtis Act decreed that each Cherokee would be given his or her own plot of land, which was called an allotment. Most allotments were to be limited to 160 acres, just a fraction of the large expanse required to graze cattle and ranch successfully. Because the land of the region was so dry and infertile, the allotments were unsuitable for farming.

The allotments were small by design. According to the Curtis Act, any land left over when all Cherokees had received their allotments belonged to the United States, and the government planned to open this land to settlement by whites. The Curtis Act thereby ensured that the Cherokee Nation in the West would soon be overrun by whites, just as their eastern homeland had been. Together, Clem and Will were only able to secure an allotment of 148 acres.

Always a realist, Clem saw that his ranching days were over and sold his cattle. Although he did not relish the idea of an Indian Territory full of whites, he was able to see a business opportunity in the situation. The white homesteaders were sure to bring money with them as they flooded into the area. With several partners, he decided to establish a bank in the nearby town of Claremore.

When Will returned from California, he was surprised to discover that his father was living in town and his family home had been rented to a farming family from Illinois, but at Clem's insistence he agreed to stay for a while anyway. Clem bought a few cattle and hired Will and his childhood friend Spi Trent to manage them and the old homestead.

Will never found the arrangement very comfortable. Running the small ranching operation offered none of the excitement of huge cattle drives and roundups. He also did not enjoy sharing the Rogers house with Clem's tenants. He and Spi were especially unhappy with the food the farmer's wife cooked for the young men. They missed the heavy meals of biscuits, beans, and gravy that were an important part of the cowboy life.

Soon Rogers and Spi built their own cabin. They enjoyed being on their own, eating the food they liked best, and entertaining whoever they pleased. They lived there contentedly until Rogers one day made the mistake of tying a pair of horses to a log protruding from the house. The two horses jerked forward, pulling off the entire side of the cabin. The family renting his father's house had just decided to return to Illinois, so, instead of repairing the cabin, Rogers moved back in. His sister May and her husband soon joined him.

Rogers's enthusiasm for his work remained slight. Aside from Clem's insistence, the only thing that kept Rogers in Indian Territory was roping contests. As the West was filling with settlers and fenced-in homesteads, the era of the cowboy was coming to an end, but people's fascination with cowboys—and the freedom they represented—was still strong. Roping contests, in which contestants displayed their skill at lassoing animals, drew large audiences and offered cash prizes to the most able contestants.

For Rogers, all the years of frustrating his family and teachers by constantly playing with his ropes began to pay off, and he became a regular at these contests. Even when he did not win, the new rope tricks he learned from the other contestants made the effort worthwhile.

In the summer of 1899, Rogers went to a fair in St. Louis to participate in a contest run by Zach Mulhall. Mulhall liked Rogers and his roping and offered the young man a job in his traveling troupe, which featured a "cowboy band"—60 musicians who played instruments while decked out in cowboy clothing. Rogers was hired to lend a little authenticity to the novelty act. While the rest of the band made their music, Rogers sat with them, pretending to play a trombone. In the middle of the act, Mulhall regaled the audience with stories of his cowboy

musicians' great feats of riding and roping. He then had Rogers, the only real cowboy of the bunch, stand up and do a few tricks to convince the crowd. Forever afterward, Rogers acknowledged Mulhall as the man who gave him his start in show business.

When Rogers's stint with Mulhall ended, he continued making the rounds of local fairs, coming home for brief visits in between contests. While returning from a fair in Kansas City in the fall of 1899, he got off his train at the station in Oolagah, a town a few miles from the Rogers home place. Rogers had sent away for a mail-order banjo and thought the station manager might have been holding the package for him. But at the ticket window he was surprised to see that the only person in charge of the station was a pretty young woman. Their eyes met; Rogers was about to begin to explain about the package but an uncharacteristic shyness left him silent. He turned and walked away without saying a word.

Rogers was more vocal a few days later when he met the woman again at a friend's house where they both had been invited to dinner. She was introduced to him as Betty Blake. Betty hailed from Arkansas and was in Oolagah visiting her sister and brother-in-law, who managed the train station.

In the presence of a group, Rogers felt more comfortable around Betty. He talked with her and even flirted a little. Only after dinner, however, when everyone gathered around the piano, did Betty meet the Will Rogers that her friends had told her was the funniest, liveliest boy for miles around. From Kansas City, Rogers had brought the sheet music for all the latest popular songs. In between jokes, he entertained Betty and the others by singing to them in his clear tenor voice.

For the next few months, Will Rogers and Betty saw each other frequently. After she returned to Arkansas,

Rogers was a great lover of horses and spent a good part of his life in the saddle. This photograph, taken when Rogers was around 20, shows him with his favorite horse at the time, Comanche.

they kept in touch through the mail. Rogers's letters became more affectionate as time went by. His jealousy of her other suitors also grew. In a mannered, somewhat self-pitying letter addressed to "My Dear Betty," he finally accused her of breaking his heart:

> Now Betty I know you will think [me] a Big Fool (which I am) . . . and I ought not to have got so broken up over you. But I could not help it so if you do not see fit to answer this please do not say a word about it to any one for the sake of a broken hearted Cherokee Cowboy.

To his disappointment, Betty did not respond to his tender plaint. With Betty gone and apparently out of his life, there now seemed no reason for Rogers to stay put. His boredom with life on the family ranch only made him more eager than ever for adventure. Rumors that large-scale ranching was thriving in Argentina seemed to

A rare photograph of Rogers and Betty Blake toward the beginning of their long courtship. Rogers, flashing his characteristic smile, is on the extreme right. Blake is on the front seat, supporting her chin with her black-gloved hand. The photograph was taken at a July 1906 house party.

provide an answer to the question of what he should do with his life. In Argentina, he could become a rich rancher, so successful that even his father would be impressed.

Clem was not terribly thrilled with the idea when it was proposed to him, however. Still, the older man could see that his son was not happy managing the small family ranch. For $3,000, Clem bought back the cattle he had given Rogers and, with mixed emotions, wished his son well as he left home for good.

3

AROUND THE WORLD

At 21, young Will Rogers left Indian Territory with some money, plenty of hope, and very little sense of exactly where he was going, though he told everyone he planned to settle in Argentina. Before he left, Rogers asked a friend, Dick Parris, to accompany him. Neither was sure precisely where Argentina was, but they knew it was to the south. The two figured they could board a ship bound for that country in New Orleans, Louisiana, but once there, they learned that the only ships for Argentina that anyone knew of left from New York City, 1,200 miles away. They arrived in New York late in the winter of 1902, just in time to learn that the yearly ship for Argentina had recently left. So, after a little sight-seeing, Rogers and Parris boarded a vessel for England, having been assured that they could easily book passage for Argentina from the English port city of Liverpool.

The trip to England was Rogers's first sea voyage; it was also his first experience with seasickness. He became miserably ill as soon as the ship left the harbor. Rogers wrote home that he "lasted just long enough to envy the Statue of Liberty for being in a permanent position."

The travelers decided to make the most of their brief stay in England. They visited as many sights as they

This publicity photograph shows a young Will Rogers supremely at ease in cowboy splendor, sporting leather chaps, a six-shooter, and—of course—a lariat.

could, taking in the Houses of Parliament, the Tower of London, and Westminster Abbey. Their visit coincided with celebrations and festivities being held all over London to celebrate the coronation of Edward VII, and in a letter to Clem, Rogers explained that he and Dick had caught a glimpse of the new king. "Don't think he recognized us, though," he added.

Upon finally reaching Buenos Aires in May, the two friends took a room in an expensive hotel where English was spoken—neither could speak Spanish, though Rogers was trying to learn—even though they had already spent most of their traveling money just making their circuitous way to Argentina. Having traveled first class throughout their odyssey, the expense did not greatly bother them, for they were certain that they would soon be making a fortune in the cattle business.

But on his first trip into the interior of the country, Rogers discovered that the rumors he had heard about Argentina contained a great deal of exaggeration. The land was indeed ideal for ranching, and the cattle there were huge and healthy, but the opportunities for someone like Will were slim. Jobs were few and the competition fierce; hundreds of other experienced cowboys with dreams of striking it rich had preceded him to the Argentine ranches.

Discouraged and homesick, Parris decided to return to America—even by pooling their remaining resources, the two friends could barely afford his return fare. Although he also wanted to go home, Rogers was relieved that he could not afford to return with his friend: he was too embarrassed to face Clem defeated and penniless after all his grandiose claims of the success he was going to achieve. After paying for Parris's ticket, Rogers spent the little that remained of his money on gifts for his family. He asked Parris to deliver them along with a story about how much he was enjoying South America.

Rogers wrote of the Atlantic Ocean voyage on which this photograph was taken, "I look happy but I wasnt." Prone to seasickness, Rogers never enjoyed ocean travel.

With no money for food and a park bench for a bed, Rogers needed work. In mid-June he received a tip that an Englishman was transporting hundreds of head of cattle by boat to his estate in South Africa and needed someone to take care of the animals on the passage. With his still-vivid memories of seasickness, the job held small appeal for Rogers, but he was desperate enough to sign on. He was then sick for the entire Atlantic crossing, from the moment the ship left port in South America until it anchored off South Africa. Although he had been too ill to do his job, Rogers was invited by the Englishman to stay on at his estate nonetheless; something about Rogers had rightly convinced the man that on dry land he was an adept handler of animals. He stayed for several months

as a groom for the man's thoroughbred horses, then, feeling footloose, hired out as a mule skinner.

At a town called Ladysmith, he was delighted to learn that a Wild West show, fronted by a man billing himself as Texas Jack, was playing nearby. Wild West shows had been popular in the United States for some time, and by the turn of the century they were developing an international audience as well. The shows usually featured demonstrations of sharpshooting, trick riding and roping, and often even mock battles between company members dressed up as cowboys and Indians. A few shows, such as Buffalo Bill Cody's "Wild West Show and Congress of Rough Riders of the World," were huge extravaganzas with hundreds of players. Texas Jack's Wild West show was far more modest, but it impressed Rogers, especially when he found out that Jack was, in fact, an experienced cowhand. Jack was every bit as excited to meet Rogers,

Buffalo Bill's Wild West Show, shown here in 1906, featured both Indians and cowboys. It was probably the grandest of all the Wild West shows that were such a popular form of entertainment at the beginning of the century.

for the last thing he had expected to find in his audience was a fellow cowboy.

While he and Rogers were having a spirited conversation about Texas ranching, Texas Jack asked Rogers if he knew any rope tricks. Rogers said he could do a few and, taking a rope from his new friend, performed the Big Crinoline, which ended with the performer twirling the rope around himself in a huge circle reminiscent of the hem of a wide-hooped crinoline skirt, a popular garment among frontier women. Texas Jack knew that the Big Crinoline was one of the hardest rope tricks to carry off, and as a promotion for his show he had even offered a prize for anyone who could do it successfully. Texas Jack did not tell Rogers about the prize, but he did offer him a job on the spot. Billed as the Cherokee Kid, Rogers was an instant hit.

Despite his success with Texas Jack's show, by the fall of 1903 Rogers had grown lonesome for the Indian Territory. With some money and Texas Jack's glowing letter of recommendation in his pocket—his former employee, Jack wrote, was "the champion trick rough rider and lasso thrower of the world"—Rogers planned to work his way home by continuing east, to Australia. Having gone halfway around the world, he reasoned, he might as well see the other half. In New Zealand, an island nation located to the southeast of Australia, the trick-roping and exotic persona of the Cherokee Kid, who had landed a job with the Wirth Brothers circus, were well received. The Auckland *Herald* declared that "the Cherokee Kid is a gentleman with a large American accent and a splendid skill." With eight months of such acclaim, Rogers was able to save enough money for the ocean passage to San Francisco and a train ticket from there to the Indian Territory. By the time he again set foot, in the summer of 1904, on the rugged plains that

In South Africa during his first around-the-world trip, Rogers, as the Cherokee Kid, got featured billing for the first time.

A celebration of the centenary of the 1803 Louisiana Purchase, the 1904 St. Louis World's Fair was the largest and most elaborate exposition the world had ever seen. Betty Blake was among the throngs who attended the fair, and thus she and Rogers were unexpectedly reunited.

had formed him, Rogers had traveled 50,000 miles in three years.

The ever-restless Rogers had barely returned to the Indian Territory before he was seeking new chances to leave. He got his wish when his old friend Zach Mulhall hired him on as one of 600 trick riders for his new Wild West show, which was to perform on the fairgrounds of the 1904 World's Fair in St. Louis, Missouri. The largest such exhibition ever organized, the St. Louis World's Fair sprawled over 1,400 acres, on which were displayed such new inventions as the automobile and exotic artifacts of foreign cultures, such as the rickshaw. Everything about the fair was on a grand scale; its opening on May 1, 1904, for example, was cued from the White House by President Theodore Roosevelt, who sent an electrical signal that simultaneously unfurled 10,000 colored flags.

Though Rogers's performance was as winning as ever, Mulhall's Wild West show did not live up to the grandeur of the fair. It came to a tawdry end when its proprietor was hauled off to jail after indiscriminately firing a pistol in the course of an argument with an employee and accidentally wounding two spectators.

With his great lariat skill and winning personality, Rogers quickly got a job with another, smaller Wild West show on the fairgrounds. While working there, he received a pleasant surprise: Betty Blake had been visiting a few friends in St. Louis and naturally wanted to see the great fair. Overhearing someone talking about

Rogers on his horse Comanche at the 1904 St. Louis World's Fair. This is one of the few photographs of Rogers in which his features suggest his American Indian heritage.

Rogers's performance, she had penned a note: Could she see him if he were not too busy?

Rogers invited Betty and her friends to come to that evening's performance. Much to her chagrin, for the show he donned his favorite costume from his days with the circus in New Zealand—a gaudy, skintight red velvet outfit decorated with gold braid in which he had appeared as the "Mexican Rope Artist." Amused already by her friendship with a show business performer, which they considered an undignified profession, Betty's friends began giggling uncontrollably the moment they saw Rogers's ridiculous costume, and Betty's face soon grew as red as Will's suit.

But it was Will's restlessness, not Betty's mortification, that prevented a renewal of their courtship. The day after the show, Will was summoned back to Claremore by his father, and he immediately renewed his itinerant way of life, working his way to Chicago with a succession of

At the beginning of his career, Rogers was a particular favorite with children. Here he performs for some youngsters while wearing the red velvet circus suit with gold brocade that later embarrassed Betty Blake.

western shows. The big city was a tougher place for a cowboy act, though, and Will was soon out of work. One day, while buying a ticket for one of the many Chicago shows that had refused to have anything to do with him, he overheard a stage manager explaining that he was desperate for an act, *any* act. Rogers volunteered his services and, to his great surprise, was immediately hired.

One evening while Rogers was on, a dog from an animal act ran across the stage. Instinctively, he threw his rope around the dog and hauled it back. The audience loved the stunt. The incident reminded Rogers of a suggestion Texas Jack had made for his act. Jack was convinced that the crowd wanted more than to see Rogers twirl his lariat. They wanted to see him rope *something*.

Though roping an animal on a small stage seemed at first impossible, Rogers came to believe it could be done. The more he thought about it, the more convinced he was that with just the right horse—specifically, a pony owned by Mulhall's wife—he could pull it off. Rogers bought the pony, whom he named Teddy after President Theodore Roosevelt, and began to train it back at Claremore. By that spring, Rogers was convinced Teddy was ready. Mulhall had been acquitted in a second trial and invited Rogers and his horse to join a show he was taking to New York City, where horse and rider made their debut at Madison Square Garden on April 27, 1905. Their first performances were warmly received, but the act did not garner real publicity until a couple of weeks into its run, when, one night, an enormous steer bolted into the audience during Zack's sister Lucille Mulhall's segment of the show. Pandemonium ensued as Lucille and several cowboys tried and failed to rope the runaway animal. Then, according to the New York *Herald*, "the Indian Will Rogers . . . headed the steer off" and "roped [its] horns." Rogers was now portrayed in the papers not only as a star performer but as a hero.

Rogers made the most of the publicity. He sent his clippings to Clem and to Betty, hoping for their approval, and to booking agents, hoping to land a better job in vaudeville, which seemed to hold a more promising future for a young performer than Wild West shows, the popularity of which was beginning to wane.

In the first decade of the 20th century, more than 2,000 theaters across the United States booked vaudeville acts. In the past, many vaudeville troupes had been known for their raunchy humor, but vaudeville shows were now trying to rise above their old risqué reputation. With the new interest in more sophisticated entertainment, few booking agents wanted to take on a folksy cowboy performer, no matter how many newspaper clippings touting his accomplishments he could show them.

Despite continuous rejection, Rogers kept asking agents for work. One finally got so fed up with him that he said he would book Rogers at the Union Square Theater if the performer would just leave him alone. Rogers was happy to take the job, even though it meant playing to the dinner crowd, traditionally the toughest audience to please. To everyone's surprise, he was a hit and played at the Union Square for a week in June.

His success there landed him a far better job at the Paradise Roof, part of the renowned Victoria Theater. Rogers was concerned about his horse's well-being— Teddy had to ride the elevator to the rooftop theater—but he was pleased with the notices his work received. He began his act at the Paradise by riding Teddy, who was fitted with specially made felt boots for traction, onto the stage. Rogers then dismounted and performed a few of his best rope tricks to music provided by the show's orchestra. His performance at the Paradise always ended with the Big Crinoline. Before swinging the rope, Rogers had an usher grab one end and stretch it out so the crowd could see its length—90 feet. Jokes were not yet a part of his performance, which was known in show business lingo as a "dumb act" in that he was not expected to speak. "The novelty of his act," the *Herald* declared, "lies in the dexterity and oddity of what he does, and the whole makes a charming specialty well out of the ordinary run." Rogers did not neglect to send Betty his best reviews.

Rogers did not remain mute onstage for long. One of the most difficult tricks he performed onstage involved roping Teddy and his rider simultaneously as they moved past him. The stunt was incredibly difficult—one rope went around the horse's neck, another encircled the rider's torso—yet it rarely elicited an exceptional audience response. The rider, Rogers's friend Buck McKee, told him that he thought the audience did not understand the skill involved. McKee suspected that the trick was performed so quickly that the audience could not even see what Rogers had accomplished. He suggested that if Rogers introduced the trick by telling the crowd exactly what they were about to see, the audience would then be more able to appreciate his feat.

Acting on his friend's advice, Rogers introduced the stunt one night by announcing what he intended to do and added, "I don't have any idea I'll get it, but here goes." Charmed, the audience laughed at his humility. Rogers performed the trick, then stormed offstage in a rage, believing that the audience had been laughing at him. But once his wounded pride had healed, he reconsidered and decided that a little talking did help his act after all.

His success in New York enabled Rogers to get vaudeville work in other places, and soon he was on the road constantly. He traveled to Philadelphia, Boston, and other cities, and from each of these metropolises he sent newspaper articles about his performances to Betty. In the spring of 1906, he took his act to Europe, where he played such glittering capital cities as Paris and Berlin, but to his profound disappointment, Betty chose not to come along, despite his invitation for her to "see the world as the *wife* of Rogers the Lariat Expert." The two met again in Claremore, where Rogers returned for a visit after the conclusion of his European tour, and then at Betty's home in Rogers, Arkansas, where Rogers stopped off on his way back to New York City. This time he proposed in person, but Betty again refused him. Though he was making almost $200 a week—a huge salary for the time—and his act was booked up for months, she saw little security in a future as a performer's wife. Rogers stormed off, determined to forget about her once and for all.

Rogers's resolution proved difficult to keep. For the next year and a half, as he played a circuit that took him to every major city in the country, Rogers kept writing his old girlfriend, even when she did not answer. Though his career was going well, he began to reconsider show business as a way of life: if it was what it took to win Betty, perhaps settling down would not be so bad. Performing was "nice work," he said, but he was not "in love with it." Still, despite the constant, grueling travel, it sure "beat that old farm and ranch and store thing."

In October 1908, with a rare unbooked week on his hands, Rogers decided to go to Arkansas and settle things with Betty. Frustrated with their long, unsettling courtship—it had now lasted eight years—he told her point-blank that she had to go back to New York with him. Though somewhat startled by the gentle Will's demand, Betty relented. Will Rogers was ecstatic. "The day I roped Betty was the greatest performance of my life," he would often declare in later years. The two were finally married on November 23, 1903, at her home in Rogers.

Will and Betty's honeymoon was a working holiday, for he had been signed for a tour that would take him to theaters all across the country for months. When the

tour ended, the couple planned to make their home in the new state of Oklahoma, which encompassed the former Indian Territory. Rogers was not sure what he would do to make a living there, but he had more or less resigned himself to the end of his performing career.

On tour, Rogers's two acts a day lasted about 40 minutes, so he had an abundance of time to spend with Betty. Rogers had been so many places that few sights held much excitement for him alone, anymore, but with Betty, who had traveled little, he found new excitement in every town and city they visited, seeing every old sight anew through Betty's eyes. In turn, Betty surprised herself by how much she enjoyed show business life. She quickly learned to love the excitement of finding herself in a new place every day and having the chance to share it all with her new husband. When the job ended, Rogers was offered another tour at a much higher salary. He and Betty agreed that he should take it.

In every city Rogers played, the newspapers raved about his act. With such acclaim, he decided that maybe it was time to start a show of his own. Slowly, he assembled a company of performers, mostly female trick riders. Rogers had no difficulty in booking his show, but he soon found that the salaries for his large cast along with the costs of transporting them and all their animals were a colossal financial drain. He lost money with each date they played, and in a short time he had no choice but to break up the show.

It was time for Will Rogers to rethink his career. He realized that he was a failure as an entrepreneur, but as

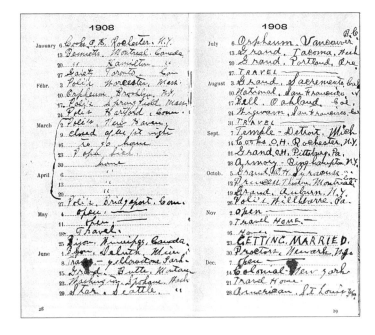

Rogers's busy engagement book reflects his hectic show business schedule, though he did manage to set aside some time on November 23 for "GETTING MARRIED."

a performer he had always been successful. A comment that a theater manager had made to Betty about his act kept coming back to him. The manager had asked her why Rogers was traveling with a company of performers when he "would rather have Will Rogers alone than that whole bunch put together." Rogers decided that the manager was right: he was at his best when he was completely on his own. He shipped his Teddy home and from then on vowed to go onstage with nothing but his ropes.

The only "props" Rogers used after that were his lariats and his voice. The embarrassment he felt in speaking onstage came to an end when he recognized that it was his gentle wit, rather than his rope tricks, that elicited the best response from his audiences. His best jokes came spontaneously from unexpected situations. One night, when performing a simple trick that involved jumping inside the circle of a twirling rope, he missed and broke the lasso. As he prepared to redeem himself by doing the trick again, he told the crowd, "Well, got all my feet through but one." The audience's laughter convinced him to make the routine a regular part of the act, missing on purpose so he could deliver his punch line.

He faced one of his toughest audiences at Chase's Opera House in Washington, D.C., in 1911. Clem and two of his daughters, Sallie and Maud, were in town and wanted to see exactly what young Will did to earn his big paycheck. Clem enjoyed the show, but, ever the businessman, delighted even more in the number of customers who had paid to see his boy. He proudly told his daughters that the theater manager was making plenty of money off Will. After traveling around the world once and across the country countless times, Rogers finally had earned what he always wanted most—his father's respect.

4

A FOLLIES STAR

By 1915, Rogers had become a staple of the vaudeville circuit. He had no trouble getting jobs, and his act inevitably drew raves from the critics and the public alike. Recognition and good pay were not quite enough for Rogers, however, for he quickly grew bored doing the same type of act over and over. A man of tremendous energy, Rogers always had to have new challenges in order to maintain the level of concentration he needed to be at his absolute best as a performer.

Rogers took his problem to one of his closest friends, actor Fred Stone. Stone agreed that Rogers's career was at a standstill and gave him one piece of advice: stay in New York City. Stone was convinced that Rogers would go nowhere so long as he was constantly traveling, playing a different theater every night. What Rogers needed, advised Stone, was a part in a Broadway musical, which was considered a more reputable form of entertainment than vaudeville.

Although Rogers had difficulty envisioning himself as a Broadway actor, he did recognize that it would provide him and his growing family with a more settled existence. He and Betty had taken a house on Amityville, Long Island, and he now had three children to provide for: William Vann, Mary, and James.

An example of Florenz Ziegfeld's "glorification of the American girl," as he characterized his artistic aim in staging the Ziegfeld Follies. *The job of Rogers and other comedians Ziegfeld employed was mainly to keep the audience entertained while Ziegfeld's show girls changed costumes.*

Rogers landed roles in a few musicals; though none ran long enough to showcase his talents effectively, he had confidence that eventually the right show would come along. His patience paid off when he received a telegram from Gene Buck, assistant to the legendary Florenz Ziegfeld. Buck wanted to hire Rogers for a two-week stint at *Ziegfeld's Midnight Frolic*, one of the most sophisticated and popular shows in New York.

The *Frolic*, which began precisely at the stroke of midnight, featured a huge cast of between 50 and 75 performers, but Rogers stood out even in this crowd. Although Ziegfeld had launched the careers of some of the greatest comedians of his time (among them W. C. Fields and Fanny Brice), he did not appreciate comic acts and included as few as possible in his shows. Sandwiched between dance numbers featuring beautiful women in outlandishly ornate costumes, Rogers's appearance constituted quite a change of pace for the audience.

Rogers's act would have seemed unconventional even if he had been surrounded by other comics. Most comics of the day told a few long stories, repeating them night after night, but Rogers took his comedic themes from the day's newspapers, and his 12-minute routine was invented anew daily. In it, he invariably touched on scores of topics and ad-libbed dozens of topical quips.

The style of Rogers's humor set him apart as well. Other comic performers told stories that built up to one punch line, hoping their audience would reward them with a big laugh. Rogers's jokes—comments and observations, really, told in a comic manner—were more subtle, designed to elicit an entirely different response: a smile or chuckle of recognition. In later years, Rogers described his comedic style:

> I use only one set method in my little gags, and that is to try to keep to the truth. Of course you can exaggerate it, but what you say must be based on truth. Personally, I don't like the jokes that get the biggest laughs, as they are

generally as broad as a house and require no thought at all. I like one where, if you are with a friend, and hear it, it makes you think, and you nudge your friend and say, "He's right about that."

Rogers's stage presence perfectly complemented his gentle brand of humor. He spoke to his audience in a calm voice, as though he were imparting his wisdom to an intimate friend rather than to a roomful of paying customers, and he never resorted to the exaggerated mugging that was the hallmark of more physical comedians. His gentleness and likability allowed Rogers to talk about subjects other comics were afraid to mention. The more abrasive W. C. Fields once recalled how one night, after the papers had reported a disturbing rash of suicides in New York City, Rogers told his audience, "They'll have to condemn the Brooklyn Bridge. . . . It's been weakened by suicides jumping off." To Fields's surprise, the crowd laughed. "If I had told it," the misanthropic star remarked, "they would have mobbed me. [Rogers] can get away with anything."

Rogers's two weeks with the *Frolic* turned into several months, after which Buck asked Rogers to join Ziegfeld's premier show, the *Follies*. At last Buck was giving Rogers the break he had been waiting for. The *Ziegfeld Follies* was the most famous stage show in the country, possibly in the world. As Rogers himself wrote, "People never spoke about [it] in comparison to any other show. It was always, 'It's better than the last year's, or it's not so good as last year's.' The Follies always stood alone."

Understandably, Buck was stunned when Rogers refused the offer. If he joined the *Follies*, Rogers explained, he would have to travel again when the show went on its annual tour. Besides, Betty felt that Ziegfeld was not paying Rogers what he was worth.

Rogers almost immediately regretted his gutsy decision. Out of curiosity, he and Betty went to the *Follies'* new spring show the night it opened. To Will's horror,

the show was awful. As always, the women were lovely and the costumes spectacular. The extravaganza, however, was dull. Rogers knew that if he were on the stage, he could breathe life into the boring show. He left the theater in misery, convinced he had lost his one chance to become a star.

Betty Rogers takes the Rogers children for a ride in a pony cart on the grounds of the family home in Amityville, Long Island.

Luckily, Ziegfeld had had exactly the same reaction to the show. The producer did not understand Rogers's humor, but he knew that his audience did. Ziegfeld himself called Rogers, asking him to reconsider. This time, Rogers had no trouble saying yes.

Both Ziegfeld and Rogers had been right. His act was exactly what the show needed. The critics gave Will the best notices of his career so far. He quickly became a headliner, an honor that helped offset the hard work involved in doing so many performances. While he was emerging as a *Follies* star, Rogers continued to play the *Frolic* nightly as well as two matinees a week. This meant he had to come up with new material for each and every performance, sometimes as many as three shows a day. As his comedy was based on current events, he claimed to "buy more newspaper extras than any man in the world."

Despite his success, Rogers remained unhappy about having to leave town and take the show on the road. He loved his family and his Long Island home. When he was not working, he spent as much time as possible teaching his children how to ride and rope at stables nearby. When Rogers told Ziegfeld he did not want to tour, the producer responded with an amazing proposal. In order to persuade Rogers to travel with the *Follies*, Ziegfeld offered him a two-year contract, wherein Rogers would make $600 a week for the first year and $750 for the second. For the time, the pay was enormous, much too good for Will to pass up, but he insisted that he did not need a contract. He trusted Ziegfeld's word, he explained, and assumed the producer trusted him.

Rogers with the chorus of the Ziegfeld Follies. *His essential role at the* Follies *never seemed to change: a down-to-earth cowboy with a lasso among lots of beautiful women. The most important change in Rogers's career came when he became known more for his humor than for his ability with a rope.*

While on tour with the *Follies*, Will had one of the most frightening experiences of his stage career. The cast was about to begin a benefit performance in Baltimore, Maryland, when a rumor spread that President Woodrow Wilson was going to attend. The news sent Rogers into a panic. The United States was about to enter World War I, and the army's lack of preparation had become one of Rogers's favorite targets. But it was one thing to criticize Wilson to the regular *Follies* audience; it was certainly another to make jokes about the president's policies to his face. For one of the few times in his performing life, Rogers was struck with a severe case of stage fright.

That night, Rogers almost had to be shoved onstage. Finding it hard to speak, he finally choked out, "I'm kinder nervous here tonight." He later admitted that his opening comment "was not an especially bright remark" but that "it was so apparent to the audience that I was speaking the truth that they all laughed heartily at it." Having broken the ice with his audience, a reassured Rogers launched into his act, forgetting about Wilson's presence long enough to make his accustomed jabs at the government. On the military's inadequacies, he said, "There is some talk of getting a Machine Gun if we can borrow one. . . . If we go to war we will just about have to go to the trouble of getting another Gun." All eyes turned toward the president, who, to everyone's (especially Rogers's) relief, laughed loud and long. Wilson later wrote with appreciation that "Will Rogers's remarks are not only humorous, but illuminating."

Offstage, Rogers took World War I very seriously. In May 1917, after the United States had entered the conflict, he pledged to donate 10 percent of his income to the American Red Cross for the duration of the war. In a letter to the president of that organization, he wrote that he wished he "had greater wealth so that I could

*Rogers supported the U.S.
effort in World War I by
pledging to donate 10 percent
of his income to the American
Red Cross in order to help
wounded American servicemen.*

give a larger amount" and explained that "if not for the
fact I owe an obligation to three little children at home,
I certainly would have been over there myself."

One of Rogers's favorite subjects emerged after the
war, when the victors became embroiled in seemingly
endless bickering over the peace settlement that was to
be imposed. While the United States indulged in an orgy
of patriotic display and homecoming parades for its
returning servicemen, Rogers felt that the real problems
of the veterans were being overlooked. "As long as they
can find a new Street in a Town that [a soldier] hasent

marched down yet," Americans would continue to hold parades for the soldiers, he said; but, as he pointed out, "they [the returning veterans] don't want to parade, they want to go home and rest." He added, "If we really wanted to honor our Boys why don't we let them sit on the reviewing stands and make the people march those 15 miles?" (Though he was well educated and intelligent, Rogers often intentionally used faulty grammar and punctuation for comic effect and to accentuate his cowboy persona.) The real challenge, as Rogers saw it, was not organizing parades but finding a way for the returning soldiers to make a livelihood. "If the money spent on stands and Parades, and the high prices people paid for the seats, had been divided up amongst the soldiers they would have had enough to live comfortably on until the next war," he said.

Rogers's jokes about the war's aftermath and the peace negotiations were so popular that in 1919 they were collected into a book—*Roger-isms: The Cowboy Philosopher on the Peace Conference*. The comedian who began as a lasso artist had now become an author.

In the same year, Rogers published a second volume, *Roger-isms: The Cowboy Philosopher on Prohibition*. In his act, Rogers had long expressed contempt for Prohibition, the U.S. policy, outlined in a 1919 amendment to the Constitution, that forbade the making, selling, and drinking of alcohol. To Rogers, the decision to drink liquor or not was entirely personal, and the government had no business trying to make that decision for its citizenry. With a trace of seriousness, he maintained the Bible was full of arguments against Prohibition. After quoting a line about Noah from Genesis ("And he drank of the wine and was drunken and was within his tent"), Rogers wrote:

> Now Noah was a chosen man. . . . If the Lord dident punish him, where do the prohibitionists come in to tell

somebody what to do? . . . Now Noah knew more about water than all of them put together. . . . He was the first man to discover a use for it, that was to float a boat on. . . . But as a beverage he knew it was a total failure.

In 1918, Rogers embarked on still another new career, that of film actor. Like so many other of his professional pursuits, his first involvement in film occurred almost by happenstance. That summer, he and Betty were having lunch with Fred Stone's sister-in-law, Edith. Her husband, Rex Beach, worked for Samuel Goldwyn, who had just formed a movie company. Beach was one of a stable of New York novelists Goldwyn had hired to write film scripts. Previously, most films had been produced without any script at all: the actors and the director generally made up the story as they filmed it. Goldwyn wanted to usher the movie industry, then in its infancy, into a new era by making movie plots more polished and sophisticated.

Beach had convinced Goldwyn to let him adapt one of his published novels, *Laughing Bill Hyde*, for the screen. Upon meeting Will Rogers, Edith Beach decided that he

Rogers in his first film, Laughing Bill Hyde. *The future film star said of his film debut that he was "an actor all right. The worst in the world."*

was the only person who could play the lead character, a happy-go-lucky tramp. Her husband and his boss immediately agreed. The only person who needed any persuading was Rogers himself. He did not feel comfortable with the idea of playing a part conceived by someone else or performing without an audience. Ultimately, however, the excitement of doing something entirely new won Rogers over, and he signed up for the picture.

Laughing Bill Hyde proved to be a money-maker as well as a critical success. The reviewer for the *New York Times* went so far as to declare that "the real Will Rogers is on the reels." Rogers's evaluation of his performance was less enthusiastic. When Goldwyn offered Rogers a two-year contract at twice his *Follies* salary, the humorist balked, saying that he was no actor. Goldwyn then took Will to a projection room and made Rogers watch *Laughing Bill Hyde* to prove him wrong. Will came out admitting that he was "an actor all right. The worst in the world."

But once again, family considerations forced Rogers to rethink his career path. Betty had just given birth to a fourth child—Frederick, named after Fred Stone—and she agreed with her husband that California would be an ideal place to raise their children. In the spring of 1919, they packed up and moved west.

During the making of Will's second movie with Goldwyn, disaster struck the Rogers family. All three boys came down with diphtheria. The two oldest, Bill and Jim, were strong enough to survive the disease, but the infant Freddie succumbed. Desperate to put their sorrow behind them, the grieving parents moved out of their house in Hollywood and bought a new home in Beverly Hills.

Over the next two years, Will went on to make 13 movies for Goldwyn. Though Rogers never changed his opinion about his skill as an actor, he did enjoy the process

Never so happy as when he had a lasso in hand, Rogers takes some time out from shooting a film on a studio lot to practice some of his rope tricks.

of filmmaking. For many of his films, he reworked the script or wrote the dialogue on the titles, the words that appeared on the screen during silent films to help explain the action. (Films were silent until 1927, nine years after Rogers made his first movie for Goldwyn.) By adding his words to the film, he was able to give his own characteristic stamp to whatever role he was playing.

Although Rogers's films were successful at the box office, his contract with Goldwyn was not renewed. Wanting to stay in California, Will decided to go out on his own and founded his own movie company. Acting as the producer, director, writer, and star, he made three films—*Fruits of Faith, The Ropin' Fool,* and *One Day in 365.* The most successful was *The Ropin' Fool,* in which Rogers performed more than 50 rope tricks. Obviously proud to have a document of his unparalleled roping skill, he later told an audience, "I don't think you might consider the [roping] Art, but there is 30 years of hard practice in it."

Although entertaining, none of the pictures Rogers produced were hits. After just three unsuccessful movies, he was dangerously close to bankruptcy. Recalling his earlier failure as a show producer, Rogers swore that this would be the last time he would ever try to be a businessman. He left Betty and the children in Beverly Hills and headed back to New York. There, at the *Follies,* he would try to recoup the family's fortunes by doing what he knew he did best—making people laugh.

5

▼▼▼

I NEVER MET A MAN
I DIDN'T LIKE

Rogers bangs out one of his newspaper columns. A typewriter soon became as essential to his well-being as a lariat.

Back in New York, Rogers took up his old job as a *Follies* star. Though his salary was good, it was not enough to pay off the debts left over from his film company, keep up with the mortgage payments on the Beverly Hills house, and finance frequent visits by Betty to the East and trips home to see his children in the West. Still, as in the past, Will Rogers was easily able to find a new audience happy to pay for a chance to hear his wit and wisdom. He became an after-dinner speaker, performing at events held by all kinds of organizations and associations in the New York area. With Rogers on the program, events always sold out. He was soon booking speaking engagements three or four nights a week, receiving about $1,000 for each appearance. Rogers joked that after a year on this hectic schedule he "had spoken at so many banquets that when I get home I will feel disappointed if my wife or one of my children don't get up at dinner and say, "We have with us this evening a man who, I am sure, needs no introduction.""

On October 26, 1922, Rogers gave a speech that would lead him to still another career. At a rally for a congressional candidate, Ogden Mills, he poked fun at all politicians and Mills in particular. Rogers later recalled that Mills sat stone-faced throughout his talk, apparently unable to tell "whether I was for him or against him." The speech may not have sat well with the candidate, but it struck a chord with many others. The editors of the *New York Times* found it amusing enough to reproduce in its entirety. V. V. McNitt, the owner of the McNaught Newspaper Syndicate, read Rogers's wry observations and appreciated his sharp wit and unique style. Reasoning that if *he* enjoyed reading Rogers's speech in the newspaper other people would as well, McNitt hired Rogers to write a weekly column, which his syndicate sold to papers across the country.

The subject for each piece was entirely up to Rogers, and as usual he had no trouble finding things in the news that he wanted to comment on. He often wrote about politics: "The more you read and observe about Politics, you got to admit that each party is worse than the other. . . . The one that's out always looks the best." Although his father was a banker, the banking industry was another of the comedian's favorite victims: "If you think [banking] ain't a Sucker Game, why is your Banker the richest man in your Town? . . . Why is your Bank the biggest and finest building in your town?"

The most obvious target for Rogers's barbs was the new president, Warren G. Harding. Soon after Harding's election in 1920, allegations emerged that many of the key people in his administration were embezzling government funds. The growing scandal carried with it enormous ramifications, yet nothing so angered the president as one of Rogers's columns, which appeared in April 1923. The article took the form of a letter to Harding in which Rogers asked to be considered for a post as an ambassador. At the end of the letter, he wrote: "Now, as to Salary, I will do just the same as the rest of the Politicians—accept a small salary as Pin Money, AND TAKE A CHANCE ON WHAT I CAN GET." To Rogers's delight, his columns soon became controversial, as the people he criticized in his understated, gentle manner began to complain about his barbs.

Soon after, Rogers left the *Follies*. He had been offered another chance in film by Hal Roach, a producer of slapstick comedies. Welcoming the opportunity to live with his family again, Rogers departed for California. Working with Roach, however, was far less to his liking. Roach's taste for broad, physical comedy held no appeal for Rogers. After making two pictures where all he had to do was "run around barns and lose my pants," he insisted that he wanted more input in the films in which he starred.

His next movie, *Two Wagons—Both Covered*, was largely his creation. Intended as a takeoff of an earlier

Rogers practices one of his most difficult lasso stunts, the Big Crinoline, on his children.

The 1924 Republican Convention, which Rogers covered as a newspaper columnist. Politicians were perhaps the most frequent target of Rogers's wit. Although he cloaked his political commentary in humor, Rogers's skill with satire allowed him to make incisive observations on the nature of politics.

film titled *The Covered Wagon,* Will played two parts and worked closely with the director on the script. The movie was a great success, but with humor far less obvious than the pie-in-the-face shtick the Roach studio executives felt comfortable producing, it did not convince Roach to give Rogers any more control over his future projects. Though Rogers fulfilled his commitment to work for Roach for two years, he performed his acting duties in his other Roach comedies with little enthusiasm.

Just as Rogers's obligation to Roach ended, McNitt approached Rogers with a new proposal. He wanted Rogers to go as a reporter to the upcoming political conventions that would select the candidates for the 1924 presidential election. Rogers was thrilled. Politics had always fascinated him. He was flattered that he was being asked to provide an official, if humorous, commentary on the most important events in the political process.

The first convention that he attended—the Republican party's—was something of a disappointment. There was little for the delegates to discuss because it was obvious who the Republican candidate would be. In August 1923, before all the scandals in his administration had been uncovered, Harding had died suddenly of a heart attack. His vice-president, Calvin Coolidge, had then assumed the presidency. With almost no competition for the nomination, Coolidge was chosen by the delegates to run for the nation's highest elected office.

Rogers had a better time at the Democratic convention, which provided him plenty of material to lampoon. The political speeches went on for days even though it was clear that they had no candidate who could make much of a showing against Coolidge on election day. On the ninth day of deliberations, Rogers used his weekly article

This 1925 show bill, used to promote a lecture tour, proclaimed Rogers "America's Greatest-Humorist." The poster's purpose was to publicize a lecture tour. Rogers's self-effacing, down-to-earth humor made him an exceedingly popular draw with banquet audiences.

AMERICA'S GREATEST HUMORIST

WILL ROGERS

THE PRINCE OF ENTERTAINERS AND ENTERTAINER OF "THE PRINCE"

Management,

Charles L. Wagner.

25¢

to propose his own Democratic candidate—Calvin Coolidge. In his estimation, if the Democrats wanted to regain the White House, they ought to get behind Coolidge because he was the only man who had a chance of winning.

Once Rogers's stint as a political reporter ended, he returned to the banquet circuit. Between October 1925 and April 1926, he delivered more than 150 talks around the country. For most people, the pace of Rogers's banquet tour would have been exhausting, but Rogers's stamina seemed to feed on the enthusiasm of his audiences. His schedule only became more demanding when, in the spring of 1926, the popular magazine *Saturday Evening Post* sent him to Europe to write a series of columns as a "Self-Made Diplomat to His President." (A collection of the columns was published later that year under the same title.) Even while traveling most of the time with Betty and the children, Rogers was able to make appointments with many of the greatest dignitaries of Europe, including the king of Spain, the Prince of Wales, and Benito Mussolini, then dictator of Italy. One luminary he did not meet was Leon Trotsky, the Russian revolutionary. Rogers had arranged to speak with Trotsky, but to his disappointment the legendary Bolshevik failed to show up for their appointment. Rogers wrote that many people had told him that he would not like Trotsky, but he had wanted to meet the man to see for himself. He explained that, politics aside, he had "never met a man I didn't like."

While in England, Rogers had an audience with Lady Astor, the first female member of the British Parliament. He was pleased to discover that her famous graciousness extended even to a visitor from Claremore, Oklahoma. After the meeting, he sent a telegram to his friends at the *New York Times*, asking that they take "good care"

Some of the targets of Rogers's gibes found him less than amusing. At a 1926 dinner of the Old Trail Drivers Association in San Antonio, Texas, Rogers's quips about white ranchers and cattle drivers stealing Indian cattle did not sit well with one member of the group, who angrily confronted him.

of Lady Astor on a trip she was planning to make to the city. "She is the only one over here who don't throw rocks at American tourists," he added.

The publisher at the *Times* was so amused that he not only printed Rogers's telegram verbatim but also demanded that he submit more. Throughout the rest of his European tour, Rogers fired off daily telegrams directly to the newspaper. They quickly became so popular that the McNaught syndicate began placing them in papers all over the country. Eventually, Rogers's telegrams would appear in more than 500 American newspapers every day.

In the end, the daily telegram may have been the best medium for communicating Rogers's wit. Unlike his weekly articles, the telegrams were short enough to allow him to concentrate on one topic. In essence, the daily telegram was the print equivalent of the little snippets of wisdom that had long delighted Rogers's *Follies* audiences.

For the rest of his life, no matter where he was, Rogers submitted a daily telegram to the McNaught syndicate. To meet his deadline, he had to deliver his piece to the local telegraph office by one o'clock in the afternoon. Every morning, Will would read a collection of papers, mulling over the news to find the right subject. When an idea struck him, he would grab his battered typewriter (one of the few possessions he carried with him on all his travels) and quickly pound out his thoughts. Rogers's newspaper pieces served several purposes. Some telegrams and articles were merely meant to entertain, but Rogers did not hesitate to use them as a soapbox through which he tried to bring the attention of his huge audience to causes that he was afraid would otherwise be overlooked. In the spring of 1927, for instance, he wrote passionately about the plight of people suffering the consequences of an unexpected flooding of the Mississippi River valley. Even though the flood had caused millions of dollars worth of damage, President Coolidge announced that the flood victims would not receive any assistance from the government. In the president's view, providing such relief was the duty of private charities. The Red Cross had been mobilized but was sorely lacking in funds: according to its estimates, the charity needed at least $5 million in emergency donations. Although Rogers was critical of Coolidge's stance, he rallied around the Red Cross, asking his readers to contribute anything they could. In one telegram, he urged whites to put aside any prejudice they might have against black flood victims:

> Look at the thousands and thousands of Negroes that never did have much, but now its washed away. You don't want to forget that water is just as high up on them as it is if

Rogers was one of the nation's earliest and most fervent supporters of aviation. Here he is seen about to take flight with Brigadier General Billy Mitchell, the country's leading exponent of air power, whose criticism of his army and navy superiors for neglecting the benefits of air power led to his court-martial.

they were white. The Lord so constituted everybody that no matter what color you are you require about the same amount of nourishment.

Rogers used the daily telegram as a forum just to air whatever was weighing on his mind. On May 21, 1927, he wrote:

> No attempt at jokes today. An old slim tall bashful, smiling, American boy is somewhere out over the middle of the Atlantic ocean, where no lone human being has ever ventured before.

The boy was 25-year-old Charles Lindbergh, who was in the process of becoming the first person to fly an airplane across the Atlantic. Like many Americans, Rogers regarded Lindbergh as a great hero. Rogers's trip to Europe, where commercial aviation was flourishing, had rekindled a long fascination with airplane flight as a means of transportation, and he frequently voiced his discontent with the U.S. government's refusal to recognize aviation's importance to America's future.

In the United States, Rogers traveled by air whenever he could, but airline accommodations were far less comfortable than those he had experienced on European commercial airlines. Usually, Rogers had to travel in U.S. mail carriers, with a stack of mail bags on his lap. Before each flight, he was weighed as though he were a package to determine his fare. On at least one occasion, he literally stuck postage stamps on himself so he could fly as air mail.

In 1927, Rogers received a peculiar invitation. Dwight Morrow, Coolidge's ambassador to Mexico, wanted Rogers to make a goodwill tour to the United States's southern neighbor. Will had long been critical of the United States's belligerent relationship with Mexico, going as far as to write that Mexico "has got her problems and we are most of them." Even so, he eagerly accepted Morrow's

Rogers was so popular with the American people by the time of the 1928 presidential elections that, as a gag, Life magazine nominated him for president. When he "lost" the election, Rogers sent the following telegram to Herbert Hoover, the winner: "Congratulations on your great victory. You will be a fine president. As for me I would rather be right."

offer, largely because his hero Charles Lindbergh was to accompany him on the tour.

By all accounts, Rogers was popular with the Mexican people. One American observer recalled that he "was all over the place making jokes, very impertinent, making fun of everybody and getting away with it." His interpreter probably helped inspire Rogers's warm reception. The translator, a clever man himself, was so adept at translating Rogers's jokes into Spanish that they retained all their subtlety and spirit.

Still, the ambassador's wife was concerned about Rogers's official role in Mexico. She knew he was a popular humorist, but she feared that, traveling with Lindbergh, who was now an international celebrity himself, Rogers was bound to be embarrassed by the lack of attention he would get. An official dinner at which the Cherokee comedian was the speaker changed her mind. As she recalled,

> From the first sentence he held the whole room in the hollow of his hand. I had entirely underestimated his power and his understanding of an audience. He shocked, flattered, cajoled, teased, tormented, and enchanted the guests.

Back home, Rogers's fame was confirmed by an offer to be the master of ceremonies of the most ambitious radio show yet produced. From his home in Beverly Hills, he introduced acts as the show was broadcast nationwide over 45 stations. Once, as a lark, he announced a special guest—Calvin Coolidge. Perfectly imitating the president's voice, he delivered a mock State of the Union address. The accent was so convincing that many people believed that Rogers's comic speech was actually Coolidge's. Will wrote an apology to the president, who, to his relief, reacted to the incident with extreme good humor.

Rogers's involvement with politics continued in 1928 when he again attended the major parties' nominating conventions. When Coolidge announced that he would not run for reelection, the Republicans chose Herbert Hoover as their presidential candidate and Charles Curtis as his vice-presidential running mate. Rogers was delighted by the nomination of Curtis, who, as a member of the Kaw tribe, was the first Indian to seek such a high office. "Come on Injun," he wrote, "if you are elected let's run the white people out of this country."

He was less thrilled with the Republican candidates' attitude toward the state of the country. According to them, all was well with the United States. To Rogers, however, the country's supposed prosperity was an illusion, as he explained in one column:

> No nation in the history of the world was ever sitting as pretty. If we want anything all we have to do is go and buy it on credit. So that leaves us without any economic problem whatever, except perhaps some day to have to pay for them.

Several weeks before the convention opened, *Life* magazine proposed an alternate candidate for president—

Will Rogers. Rogers gleefully went along with the
stunt, even contributing the name of his sponsors, the
Anti-Bunk party. The magazine published his campaign
platform: "If elected I absolutely and positively agree
to resign . . . that's offering the Country more than
any Candidate ever offered it in the history of its
entire existence."

Despite his levity, the 1928 campaign depressed
Rogers. Like Hoover, the Democratic party nominee,
Al Smith, seemed to have no inkling that the United
States's seeming prosperity was built on a hollow foun-
dation. While Rogers suspected that the good times
were soon going to end, each candidate insisted that
the country's good economic fortunes would continue
forever—though only, of course, if he was elected. With
a more angry tone than he usually took, Rogers railed
against the nominees' obviously false promises:

> If a speaker can convince a man that he is prosperous when
> he is broke, or that he is not prosperous when he is doing
> well . . . then his Government shouldn't be in the hands of
> the people. We might as well have candidates argue with
> us that we have a pain in our stomach.

6

HELPING A COUNTRY
IN NEED

In his March 1929 inaugural address, the new president, Herbert Hoover, told the electorate, "I have no fears about the future of our country. It is bright with hope." For most Americans, his optimism was unfounded. For Will Rogers, however, the next few years would be replete with prosperity as he took center stage as the country's most celebrated performer.

Although Rogers continued to write his daily telegrams and weekly articles, he turned his attention away from politics immediately after the election. Hollywood was once again courting him, but this time with a different lure. The film industry had learned how to attach a soundtrack to film images, and almost overnight "talking pictures" had completely replaced silent films. Old stars whose voices did not suit their images became nobodies. A celebrity such as Rogers, however, whose popularity so depended on the expert timing and inflection of the lines he delivered, was in demand more than ever.

Rogers was an immediate sensation in the talkies (or "noisies" as he preferred to call them). He had never felt comfortable trying to express himself solely in gestures, as he had been required to do in silent films. Now,

"When I die," Rogers often said, "my epitaph is going to read: 'I joked about every prominent man of my time, but I never met a man I didn't like.'"

83

however, all of what had made Will Rogers a major talent onstage could be recorded on film.

Rogers also found that his old style of working could be adapted to his new role as a star of the talkies. In the *Follies* he had read the latest edition of the newspaper right before going onstage to get ideas for his monologue. Similarly, he now took the next day's shooting script home at night and gave it a quick read. However, unlike the other actors, he never learned his lines. From years of experience, he knew that by ad-libbing he could come up with better dialogue while the cameras were rolling.

Rogers's technique usually did result in a better movie than the one scripted, but it nearly drove his fellow actors

Anything and everything was fair game for Rogers's lasso—even a steamboat, as he demonstrated in the 1935 film Steamboat Round the Bend.

insane. Actors working with Rogers never knew what he was going to say. Trying to follow the script, they would become lost when Rogers neglected to deliver the cue that signaled when they needed to speak their next line. Directors had an even more difficult time. Responsible for keeping their films to a schedule and within their budgets, they often grew impatient with Rogers, who required take after improvised take to create a scene that satisfied both the star and the director.

Despite this seemingly casual approach, Rogers always strived to give the best performance possible in his films. Although he took his role as an actor seriously, he did not take the idea of being a star seriously at all. One of the biggest box-office draws in Hollywood, he was accorded a lush dressing room in a private bungalow, but he felt uneasy in such opulent quarters. On movie sets, he usually spent his free time reading the newspapers or napping in his car. Essentially unchanged by his success, he remained humble and unpretentious in a community well known for its artificiality and its abundance of big egos.

Paradoxically, many of the people in the film industry who worked with Rogers were struck by his shyness. Actor Spencer Tracy saw him as "at the same time, one of the best-known, and one of the least-known men in the world. By inclination, he is a grand mixer; by instinct, he is as retiring as a hermit." Those even closer to Rogers agreed with this assessment of his character. As an adult, his son Jim remembered Rogers as "a loner" who had few intimate friends. Bill, Rogers's oldest child, felt that he barely knew his father, largely because Rogers was constantly traveling while he was growing up.

Rogers's entire family therefore welcomed the stability his success in sound films gave them in the early 1930s. On a large plot of land that he purchased in Santa Monica,

Rogers supervised the construction of a large house as well as adjoining stables and a polo field, where he taught his three children the game's intricacies, which he had learned on Long Island some years earlier. Between films, Rogers liked to invite any available competitors to take on the family team, until the teenaged Mary stopped playing once she, as a disappointed Rogers put it, "went social on us." Rogers took great pride in his house, which was set on a hill overlooking a beautiful valley, and he spent much of his spare time and money making improvements on it.

The constant work on the Santa Monica estate was expensive, but at this stage in his career Rogers had no

The Rogers family at home in California; from left to right are sons Bill and Jim, Betty, daughter Mary, and Will. Jim is embracing one of the family's many pets, the calf Sarah. Rogers attributed his success to his having "stayed an old country boy."

Unemployed men wait for a handout of bread in New York City during the Great Depression. Rogers was greatly frustrated by the refusal of the administration of President Herbert Hoover to allocate relief funds; when Congress refused to pass a $15 million food bill but appropriated the same amount to improve entrances to the national parks, he quipped, "You can get a road anywhere you want out of the government, but you can't get a sandwich."

trouble affording it. In 1930, he signed a contract with the Fox Film Company in which he agreed to make four pictures. For each he would earn $150,000—an astronomical sum for the time. With his pay for his film work and the income he received for his newspaper columns and telegrams, Rogers was a very wealthy man.

Most other Americans, however, were not faring nearly as well. Rogers's dire assessment about the U.S. economy had been correct. The country's supposed prosperity, all based on borrowed money, had proven to be an illusion that came to a cruel end on October 29, 1929, when the nation's stock markets crashed, plunging the nation into the greatest economic crisis in its history.

Though the causes of the Great Depression were many and complex, to Rogers the explanation for the nation's economic collapse was simple: irresponsible financial

speculation by the wealthiest segments of the nation's population. He saw playing the stock market as a form of gambling, indulged in by people who arrogantly expected to get something for nothing and had by their folly and greed undermined the nation's financial structure. "Oh, it was great while it lasted," he wrote in one column about the rampant financial speculation that had characterized the 1920s, much of which had been conducted on credit. "All you had to do was to buy and wait till the next morning and just pick up the paper and see how much you made, in print. But all that has changed. . . . Somebody has to do some work." He had little doubt that the rich would suffer the least from the great Stock Market Crash: "Be it pestilence, war or famine, the rich get richer and the poor get poorer."

Rogers was equally furious with the politicians in Washington who refused to acknowledge the extent to which the populace was suffering from the Depression. When the House of Representatives failed to approve a Senate bill that called for $15 million of federal funds to be spent on food for the poor and unemployed, Rogers wrote, "They seem to think that's a bad precedent, to appropriate money for food. It's too much like the 'dole.' They think it will encourage hunger. The way things look, hunger don't need much encouragement. It's just coming around naturally."

Like Coolidge before him, Hoover believed that providing emergency relief to the needy was not the government's responsibility. As millions of Americans in the grip of the Great Depression went hungry, he insisted that their problems would be solved if their neighbors— themselves impoverished by the troubled economy—just demonstrated charity. Hoover also maintained that private organizations were well equipped to aid the hungry.

Always interested in helping those in need, Rogers appeared at a benefit for the Children's Hospital in Boston, Massachusetts, with another popular American hero, baseball slugger Babe Ruth. Both Ruth and Rogers were known for their devotion to children and charitable causes.

Knowing this was not true, Rogers traveled to Washington in January 1931. By then possibly America's best-known entertainer, Rogers had no difficulty getting an audience with the president. Hoover told Rogers that he did not want to offer relief to America's hungry because once they received relief money from the government "they will always expect it." Rogers did not agree but realized that the president's opinions were firm. He gave up trying to change Hoover's mind and devoted himself instead to doing everything he could to assist the Red Cross's efforts to feed the hungry.

Paying all of his own expenses, Rogers immediately organized an 18-day tour that took him to 50 different cities. All the proceeds from his appearances went to the

Red Cross, although he did require that a portion of the money he raised go to the people of the Cherokee tribe. On his tour, Rogers saw firsthand how badly most Americans were faring, which only fueled his anger at the government's inaction. After visiting many remote locations, Rogers lamented that there were still some people he could not reach: "I am speaking of the Senate and Congress of these United States."

Hoover was no fan of Rogers's savage criticism, but he did appreciate his power to affect the citizenry. Knowing he needed help in carrying his message to the unhappy public, the president asked Rogers to join him on a radio show on October 18, 1931, in which he planned to ask the American people to contribute still more to charity. Though Rogers still thought that the government was neglecting its responsibilities, he agreed to appear with the president in the belief that he should do anything possible to help the people in the greatest need. During the broadcast, Rogers uttered one particularly memorable line about the strange position of mixed wealth and poverty in which the United States then found itself: "We are the first nation in the history of the world to go to the poorhouse in an automobile."

Amid his concern for his fellow citizens, Rogers never forgot the situation of Native Americans. About being Cherokee, he said, "I am a Cherokee and it's the proudest little possession I ever hope to have." At a time when most non-Indians were unaware of how cruelly the American government had treated Indians, Rogers spoke out from time to time on the injustices that had been visited upon Native Americans. In reference to the United States's many failures to honor its promises to Indians, he said, "The Government, by statistics, shows they have got 456 treaties that they have broken with the Indians. That is why the Indians get a kick out of reading the

Government's usual remark when some big affair comes up, 'Our honor is at stake.'"

On another occasion he spoke of the government's treatment of his own tribe: "They [the United States government] sent the Indians to Oklahoma. They had a treaty that said, 'You shall have this land as long as grass grows and water flows.' It was not only a good rhyme but looked like a good treaty, and it was till they struck oil. Then the Government took it away from us again. They said the treaty only refers to 'Water and Grass'; it don't say anything about oil."

When the government announced plans to build a hospital for Indians in his hometown of Claremore, Rogers immediately placed the event in the greater context of the history of U.S. treatment of Native Americans. "In speaking of Indians," he asked, "do you know that Claremore, Oklahoma, is going to open the only Indian hospital in the United States? . . . [W]e have the only one built by the Government entirely for Indians. You know Columbus discovered this country about 400 years ago or something, and it took 400 years for the Government to build a hospital for the Indians. Look what the Indians have got to look forward to in the next 400 years. They are liable to build us a cemetery or something."

The ominous international scene concerned Rogers almost as much as domestic affairs. Many of the European nations were experiencing economic disaster comparable to that of the United States, and amid the political chaos and attendant suffering, belligerent leaders, preaching messages of hatred and territorial expansion, were gaining power. With dread Rogers predicted, "War is nearer around the corner than prosperity is."

Back at home, a smaller—though highly charged— battle was already raging. After World War I, Congress had promised to give all veterans a monetary bonus for helping to defeat America's enemies. The government had long delayed relinquishing the funds, but as the Great Depression took its hold, the suffering veterans became impatient. One group of unemployed men from the Pacific Northwest decided it was time to act. They traveled across the country to Washington, D.C., determined to camp on a lawn near the Capitol until the government made good its guarantee of compensation for their wartime sacrifice.

Although Rogers did not support their march, he respected their peaceful protest, writing that "they hold the record for being the best behaved of any 15,000

Rogers often stated jokingly that he only knew what he had read in the papers—but he read a lot of them and was also well traveled. Early in his career, he formed the habit of reading several newspapers each day as a means of gathering comedy material.

hungry men ever assembled anywhere in the world." As a message to the officials of the government, he added, "It's easy to be a gentleman when you are well fed, but these boys did it on an empty stomach."

The president did not share Rogers's admiration. In June 1932, U.S. army troops, led by General Douglas MacArthur, rolled tanks into the veterans' camp. As a final indignity, the soldiers set the veterans' makeshift tents ablaze. The meaning of the gesture was clear: the plight of the common man, rocked by the country's depression, was of no concern to the government.

In this climate, Rogers's message was more potent than ever before. For years, in his speech and columns, he had championed the average American. Now, in an era when respectable citizens were being treated as criminals, Rogers appeared a center of sanity, ever willing to speak the truth.

Given the public's well-founded suspicion of professional politicians, it is not surprising that an organization of influential Californians asked Rogers to run for president in 1932. Four years earlier, Rogers had clearly expressed his reluctance: "We are used to having everything named as Presidential candidates, but the country hasn't quite got to the professional comedian stage." With more experience, Rogers's refusal to seek a government post became only more adamant. "Will you do me a favor," he wrote, "if you see or hear of anybody proposing my name for any political office, will you maim said party and send me the bill?"

7

THE FINAL ADVENTURE

Despite Rogers's refusal to be a candidate for office in 1932, he found himself at the center of still another presidential campaign season. In early June, he made an appearance at the Republican convention, which he maintained was "held for no reason at all," for it was obvious well before the delegates' votes were counted that no one would beat out "the same old vaudeville team of Hoover and Curtis" for the nomination.

Later that month, the Democratic convention provided Rogers with all the senseless, but entertaining, bickering that he so associated with politics. His second day at the convention, he summed up—with great glee—the delegates' behavior with "They fought, they fit, they split and adjourned in a dandy wave of dissension." While the various factions in the party were battling, someone got the wise idea of asking Rogers to lend a little levity to the proceedings. For 15 minutes, he held the floor, getting healthy laughs and applause from a crowd weary from too much political discussion. But Rogers, himself a Democrat, used his speech to impart to the delegates some advice that he took very seriously: once the nominee was chosen, all Democrats needed to band together and give him their support. Hoover's unpopularity almost guaranteed that his Democratic opponent could take the election

Rogers disembarks from his plane in Alaska; ace aviator Wiley Post is visible at the controls.

95

if the party supported him. As Rogers put it, if the Democratic nominee "lives until November, he is in!"

In the end, the Democratic delegates chose as their nominee Franklin D. Roosevelt, the governor of New York state. Rogers was pleased with the selection, convinced that Roosevelt was much more willing than Hoover to listen to the concerns of the Americans who were hurting the most from the Depression. He did some campaigning for the Democratic candidate, but he quickly lost his enthusiasm for the upcoming election once the two nominees began bitterly attacking one another. By the early fall, Rogers had become so tired of hearing "Hoover said this" and "Roosevelt said that" that he decided to leave the country to escape from the election news.

For several weeks in October 1932, he traveled through Chile, Argentina, and Brazil, but he returned home a few days before the election, just in time to communicate his thoughts about it in several telegrams. Many of his comments were uncharacteristically harsh. In one, he confessed to losing whatever faith he had had in the country's system for electing its leaders: "If by some divine act of providence we could get rid of both these parties and hire some good men, like any other big business does, why that would be sitting pretty." Another telegram advised Hoover and Roosevelt to stop hurling accusations at one another and instead go fishing until the votes had been counted. "You will be surprised," he told the candidates, "but the old United States will keep right on running while you boys are sitting on the bank."

Rogers was shocked by the response his words drew. Many of his readers wrote their newspapers, angered by Rogers's attacks on the candidates. Some were incensed by what they saw as Rogers's insolence in presuming to tell Hoover and Roosevelt how to behave. Taken aback by the criticisms, Rogers, for a time, took care not to offend his audience any further. After the election, the only words he had for the candidates were kind. To the defeated Hoover, Rogers said, "Cheer up. You don't know how lucky you are." To Roosevelt, he merely offered a piece of friendly advice: "Don't worry too much."

Rogers was not able to tone down his style for long. That winter, before Roosevelt's inauguration, Hoover invited the president-elect to the White House to discuss an old problem—the nonpayment of debts incurred by the United States's European allies during World War I. Rogers wrote a newspaper piece that counseled Roosevelt not to go, because the country should have one president, not two. Again, he angered readers who felt he had no right telling their future president how to do his job.

The controversy passed, largely because once Roosevelt was sworn in Rogers expressed heartfelt support for the new president. Roosevelt turned out to be exactly the type of leader Rogers thought the United States needed. Soon after the president took office, Rogers declared: "Even if what he does is wrong [the people] are with him, just so he does something. If he burned down the capitol we would cheer and say, 'Well, we at least got a fire started, anyhow.'"

Even though the hard times showed no sign of ending, Rogers sensed that all Americans were feeling more optimistic with Roosevelt in the White House. "Actual knowledge of the future was never lower, but hope was never higher," he wrote. Rogers even suspected that, in an unexpected way, the Depression itself was giving people reason to feel good about their lot: "America hasn't been as happy in three years as they are today—no money, no banks, no work, no nothing."

Still, Rogers continued to do more than his share to help those with nothing. In 1933, he agreed to make

Rogers during a radio performance for NBC. His radio talks attracted millions of faithful listeners and further contributed to his immense popularity.

seven radio broadcasts for the Gulf Oil Company, pro- vided that his fee—$50,000—would be given to the Red Cross and the Salvation Army. At the time, Rogers's popularity as a film star was greater than ever, and from 1933 to 1935 he was the nation's top box-office draw. The Gulf shows, broadcast nationwide, brought him an even larger audience. People too poor to afford movie admis- sion were eager to find friends with a radio, on which they could hear Rogers for free.

At first, Rogers did not enjoy performing on the airwaves. Just as when acting in films, he missed having a live audience whose laughter would let him know which parts of his routine were working and which parts were falling flat. Even worse was the strict time limit radio placed on his act. In the *Follies* and at his speaking engagements, Rogers had become accustomed to talking for as long as he had something to say. For the Gulf shows, he was scheduled to speak for 15 minutes, no more and no less. In his first few broadcasts, Rogers lost track of time and was cut off in mid-sentence.

Characteristically, Rogers came up with a comic solution to his problem: He brought an alarm clock to every show. Just before the beginning of his talk, he set the alarm to ring when 15 minutes had passed. His regular listeners came to expect the sound of the alarm, after which Rogers would always be able to squeeze in a hasty send-off.

Rogers's first seven broadcasts were so successful that Gulf signed him up for an additional six, and then even more. For the next two years, many American families made a point of gathering by the radio every Sunday night to hear what Will Rogers had to say that week. Thus, Rogers became the first radio commentator.

While his fame as a radio star was growing, Rogers kept up his hectic schedule of newspaper writing and film acting. He always considered writing his daily telegrams a delight, although the weekly article sometimes felt like a chore. Acting, however, never became great fun for Rogers. He had committed himself to appearing in three films for the Fox Film Company every year, but he liked to get them over with between January and June, which left him with a full six months fairly free for his favorite recreation—travel.

In the summer of 1934, Rogers decided to use his time off to take a trip around the world. He convinced Betty, Bill, and Jim to accompany him for most of the journey. They traveled extensively in Hawaii, Japan, Korea, and most of the countries of Europe.

For Rogers, the trip's highlight was Siberia, a vast, desolate area in the Russian Republic. The weather conditions were so poor that he could not travel by plane, so instead he booked passage on the Trans-Siberian Express, a train that ran across its icy terrain. Usually, Rogers did not enjoy traveling by train; he much preferred flying to his destination and then investigating the place and its people on foot. But Rogers saw something special in the wilderness he viewed from a window aboard the Express. He wrote home, "It's exactly like the Indian Territory was when I grew up in it as a boy. And if you can find a finer one than that was before they plowed and ruined it, I don't know where."

When he returned home, Rogers set about making the three movies that would fulfill his commitment to Fox for 1935. All the time, however, his mind was elsewhere. He had grown tired of the film industry and complained that he wanted to have some fun "without some director hollering at me." Betty noticed his impatience. According to Rogers, whenever he was eager to put work aside and travel, "I sorter begin to looking up in the air and see what is flying over, and Mrs. Rogers in her wise way will say, 'Well, I think you better get on one. You are getting sorter nervous.'" With the completion of his third film, in July, Rogers began to make new travel plans in earnest.

An exciting opportunity presented itself during a chance meeting with an old friend and fellow

Though Betty and Will Rogers had traveled much of the world together, she refused to accompany him to Alaska.

Oklahoman, pioneer aviator Wiley Post, who had gained fame in 1931 by flying an airplane around the world in eight and a half days. Post now planned to test the commercial viability of carrying goods from the United States to Asia by flying over Alaska and Siberia rather than the traditional, and far longer, route over the Pacific Ocean, and he invited Rogers to join him.

Rogers welcomed the opportunity to visit Siberia again, but he was attracted even more by the chance to view the pristine terrain of Alaska. He had heard many tales about the region from prospectors who had traveled there during the 1896 Klondike gold rush, and he was eager to visit Alaska himself so he could "meet the old boys that had the nerve to stick" it out in such a brutal, yet beautifully unspoiled, environment. To Will's disappointment, Betty could not share his enthusiasm. She argued that the trip would be dangerous and uncomfortable and begged him to stay home.

The two Oklahomans departed from Seattle, Washington, on August 6, 1935, in Post's makeshift plane, which he had fashioned from various spare and scavenged parts, including a recently affixed pair of pontoons that would be used for the various water landings necessary in Alaska. In flight, Rogers spent much of his time with his typewriter on his lap, tapping out his daily telegrams and weekly articles thousands of feet above the Alaskan wilderness. The serious intent of the trip was soon forgotten as the travelers, like a pair of young boys, took to heading out for whatever remote Alaskan spot appealed to them that day. To Rogers, the unpredictability of their trip made it all the more fun. "Was you ever driving around in a car and not knowing or caring where you went?" he wrote in a letter home. "Well, that's what Wiley and I are doing. We sure are having a great time. If we hear of whales or polar bears in the Arctic, or a big herd of caribou or reindeer, we fly over and see it."

There was only one spot Rogers was determined not to miss. He had long heard stories about an old trader named Charles Brower who had lived in Alaska for nearly 50 years. Now a commissioner for the U.S. government, Brower was stationed in Barrow, a remote village of only about 300 inhabitants, most of whom were Eskimos. Rogers and Wiley agreed that, if only to meet Brower, they had to add Barrow to their itinerary.

On August 15, despite reports of storms and turbulence en route, Post and Rogers left the city of Fairbanks for Barrow. Almost as soon as they were airborne, the plane ran into one of the worst storms the natives of the region had ever seen. After several hours, Post finally chanced upon a break in the clouds just large enough so that he was able to spot a lagoon where the plane could land. Fortunately for the travelers, a small Eskimo hunting and fishing camp bordered one side of the lagoon. As Post and Rogers stepped out of the plane, they were greeted by a seal hunter, Claire Okpeaha, his wife, and their son, who told them they were just ten minutes' flight from

Barrow. The men thanked the Okpeahas for their help; Rogers, as he always did when he met new people in a new place, asked the Eskimos about themselves and about what they were doing. For a few minutes, the Okpeahas told their attentive listener all about seal hunting and camp life. Post then explained that it was time they were getting along. He and Rogers climbed back in the plane, and Rogers waved good-bye to the Okpeahas as the engines started up.

Post slowly taxied the craft to one end of the small lagoon, then raced it across the icy water, lifting its nose into the air just before the pontoons met the opposite shore. The Okpeahas watched as the plane rose higher and headed in the direction of Barrow. As the Eskimos walked away to return to their fishing, they heard a sudden change in the sound of the engine—a frantic sputtering replaced its loud roar. As they turned to watch, the plane seemed to hang in the air for a moment as the engine cut. In a second, its nose fell off, and the plane zoomed downward, ending its dive in the bottom of the lagoon.

Alerted by Claire Okpeaha, who covered the 16 miles to Barrow on foot in five hours, a rescue party hurried to the site by boat, but there was no one to save. The wrecked plane bobbed slowly in and out of the water; Rogers and Post had been killed instantly when the plane struck the lagoon's sandy floor.

The crudeness of Barrow's radio equipment prevented news of the deaths from reaching the United States until the next day, but the crash was then headline news for more than a week. The *New York Times* devoted four full pages in both its Saturday and Sunday editions to the two heroes' obituaries. The grieving Betty received letters from friends and acquaintances of Rogers from around the world. Everyone who had encountered Will Rogers seemed to have a story to share about how he had touched their lives. For the many more Americans who had never met Rogers, the sorrow was just as great. Although they did not know the man personally, they knew his face, his words, his charm, and his humor. They mourned his death as they might have that of an old friend.

Will Rogers was buried at the Forest Lawn Memorial Park in Los Angeles on August 22, 1935. More than 50,000 people attended his funeral; many others came to pay their respects at memorial services held in Hollywood, Beverly Hills, and Claremore.

In 1944, Rogers's and his son Fred's remains were brought to Oklahoma. Decades earlier, Rogers had bought a plot of land on a hillside in Claremore where he always hoped to live one day. His busy life and early death prevented him from ever coming home to stay, so Betty thought it only fitting that the old Indian Territory, which he loved so much throughout his life, be the place he spend eternity. A month later, she was buried beside him.

Today Will Rogers's name and face are still well known, although his work is largely forgotten. Few

Rogers circled the world three times in his lifetime; his last journey ended in this bleak Alaskan landscape, where Eskimos gazed upon the crumpled wreckage of the plane that carried him and Post to their death in August 1935.

Will Rogers left behind him a legacy of wit, honesty, common sense, and compassion for humanity; his death occasioned perhaps the greatest outpouring of public grief in the United States since the assassination of Abraham Lincoln.

people read the collections of his writings or watch his films. Yet, even to many of those unfamiliar with the details of his career, Rogers remains a symbol of many of the treasured values that the pressures of modern times seem to have stripped from American society. He is remembered as a man who found humor in any situation, treated all people with respect, and valued truth above everything. Now, as in his lifetime, the image of Will Rogers acts as a mirror in which all Americans can see their best selves.

CHRONOLOGY

Nov. 4, 1879	William Penn Adair Rogers born in Indian Territory
1897	Leaves home to find work as a cowboy
1899	Joins a cowboy band in a traveling troupe run by Zach Mulhall; begins courtship of Betty Blake
1902–4	Rogers works his way around the world as a livestock handler and as the Cherokee Kid, lariat artist extraordinaire
1904–6	Rogers performs in Mulhall's Wild West show at the St. Louis World's Fair; tours the United States and Europe after adding topical humor to his lariat act
Nov. 23, 1908	Marries Betty Blake
1908–18	Rogers becomes the most popular onstage performer in the United States
1918–20	Makes his debut as a film actor in Samuel Goldwyn's *Laughing Bill Hyde*
1919	Two collections of Rogers's political humor are published
1920s	Becomes the most sought-after speaker on the American banquet circuit
1922	Begins writing his popular weekly syndicated newspaper column
1924	Covers the presidential nomination conventions of both major parties
1925–26	Newspapers begin syndicating his daily telegrams
1928	Makes a goodwill tour of Mexico with ace flier Charles Lindbergh
1929–32	Rogers acts in the new "talking pictures," becoming for a time the most popular male box-office star
1931	Encourages Americans to donate to charity and relief efforts concerned with alleviating the effects of the Great Depression
1933–35	Becomes a radio star through his broadcasts for the Gulf Oil Company; donates his fee to the Red Cross and the Salvation Army
1934	Travels around the world with his family
Aug. 15, 1935	Dies in a plane crash in Alaska
1944	Rogers's remains are brought home to the old Indian Territory in Claremore, Oklahoma

FURTHER READING

Alworth, E. Paul. *Will Rogers*. New York: Twayne, 1974.

Anderson, Peter. *Will Rogers, American Humorist*. Chicago: Childrens Press, 1992.

Brown, William Richard. *Imagemaker: Will Rogers and the American Dream*. Columbia: University of Missouri Press, 1976.

Day, Donald, ed. *Sanity Is Where You Find It*. Boston: Houghton Mifflin, 1955.

Ketchum, Richard M. *Will Rogers: His Life and Times*. New York: American Heritage, 1973.

Rogers, Will. *The Autobiography of Will Rogers*. New York: Avon, 1975.

Sterling, Bryan B., and Frances N. Sterling, eds. *A Will Rogers Treasury: Reflections and Observations*. New York: Crown, 1982.

———. *Will Rogers in Hollywood*. New York: Crown, 1984.

———. *Will Rogers' World*. New York: Evans, 1989.

Wayne, Bennett. *The Super Showmen*. Champaign, IL: Garrard, 1974.

INDEX

PICTURE CREDITS

LIZ SONNEBORN is a freelance writer living in New York City. The editor of many volumes for young adult readers on Native American peoples, she is the author of *The Cheyenne Indians* in Chelsea House's JUNIOR LIBRARY OF AMERICAN INDIANS series.

W. DAVID BAIRD is the Howard A. White Professor of History at Pepperdine University in Malibu, California. He holds a Ph.D. from the University of Oklahoma and was formerly on the faculty of history at the University of Arkansas, Fayetteville, and Oklahoma State University. He has served as president of both the Western History Association, a professional organization, and Phi Alpha Theta, the international honor society for students of history. Dr. Baird is also the author of *The Quapaw Indians: A History of the Downstream People* and *Peter Pitchlynn: Chief of the Choctaws* and the editor of *A Creek Warrior of the Confederacy: The Autobiography of Chief G. W. Grayson.*